RECOVERING REPENTANCE

a call to spiritual brokenness

RECOVERING REPENTANCE

a call to spiritual brokenness

John Morganti

Wicket Gate Books
Wake Forest, North Carolina

Recovering Repentance:
A Call to Spiritual Brokenness

Published by Wicket Gate Books
Wake Forest, North Carolina

Cover design by Jenny Davis, 2017
Editing and typesetting by InkSmith Editorial Services

Recovering Repentance/John Morganti.—1st ed.

ISBN: 978-0-578-42340-1

To my wife, Laura, who, like the men in 1 Samuel 30:23–25, so often "stayed with the gear" and will receive the warrior's share. Also, to the memory of the late Paris Reidhead, whose sermon "Ten Shekels and a Shirt" God used to expose my self-deception.

I would like to thank those who helped with editing and gave valuable feedback: Julie Willin, Becky Levin, Kim Booth, Dr. Allen Ferry, and Rick Smith. Many thanks also to Liz Smith of InkSmith Editorial Services for her careful editing of the manuscript.

Contents

Foreword

What you are about to read is both a travelogue of the author's salvation experience as well as a map recording how he got there. Repentance is central to both. At this writing, John Morganti was saved only four years ago, and he began writing this book almost right away. That in itself reflects something about his awareness of the significance of repentance, having so recently experienced it himself. But this should not deter the serious reader from probing these pages. The nearness of repentance with his maturity as an individual has in this sense qualified him to write with passion and clarity, and the weight of the book shows the study he put into it from the start. In fact, I would say that one of the benefits of John's book is his ease of style, like someone who is star-eyed, having just witnessed a striking event. This produces a study of repentance that is at once accessible to the novice believer while still going deep enough to reward anyone willing to pursue it further. In this regard, I appreciated the citations he culled from godly men in church history such as John Calvin, Thomas Watson, Jonathan Edwards, C. H. Spurgeon, and J. Gresham Machen, among others.

It is an honor for me to recommend John's book to you. As a pastor of over twenty-six years in the same town where he grew up, I have watched John's growth in grace with heartfelt interest. It is particularly so because of our common burden. About twenty years ago I was impressed to study the nature of true Christianity in the works of Jonathan Edwards and Thomas Boston. This subsequently became the subject of my doctoral dissertation at Gordon-Conwell Theological Seminary. So, when John and I discussed his deep concern to recover the right approach to salvation, specifically regarding repentance and seeking God, it immediately resonated with my heart.

John seeks to reclaim repentance from misguided notions of its importance and, worse, from ignorance of its necessity. To do this he lays a solid foundation for the doctrine of repentance in the first chapter by giving its biblical basis. He then discusses its consequences in chapter 2. Anticipating objections in chapter 3, he deftly keeps returning the reader back to what Scripture teaches, that true repentance demands the heart's involvement, not merely the head's. In chapter 4, it's hard for the penitent sinner not to feel relief when you read of the results of true repentance. Godly sorrow produces in the sinner both forgiveness from sin's bondage and the glorious privilege to walk in union with Jesus Christ.

Teachers and pastors will find wise guidance in chapter 5 where John directs believers to carefully navigate the unsure waters of modern evangelism. I draw special attention to his warning of what many of us were weaned on, the invitation system, and what is popularly termed "the social gospel" or "easy-believism." Though certainly not a new problem, these issues persist today because man's innate depravity, coupled with our culture's narcissistic bent, tend to spurn Christ's call to self-denial. So, we need this word in our day. Still, as John writes from a Reformed perspective he is careful to steer the reader clear of an opposite error, "works salvation." Salvation is always a work of grace from start to finish.

Now, up to chapter 6 most readers will likely be familiar with the doctrines of repentance and salvation, even if its nuances are not as well understood. But in this final chapter we discover what may seem new to many, which is the doctrine of seeking God and the call to self-examination prior to salvation. But the doctrine of seeking is not new at all. The call of Jesus, as John points out, is this: "Strive to enter through the narrow gate" (Luke 13:24). It is a study that finds one of its chief proponents in Jonathan Edwards and is dealt with in a book edited by William C. Nichols, *Seeking God: Jonathan Edwards' Evangelism Contrasted with Modern Methodologies*. John helpfully cites this important book. This chapter with the truths it proposes and the ideas that it engenders is alone well worth the price of the book.

The scope of *Recovering Repentance: A Call to Spiritual Brokenness* recommends itself to laymen, Bible students, and pastors alike. I cannot help but see how any teacher could easily adapt this material in Sunday school or small group settings. To that end, may the Lord bless these pages to the building up of Christ's own church to His own glory.

> The closer any man comes to the likeness of God, the more the image of God shines in him. In order that believers may reach this goal, God assigns to them a race of repentance, which they are to run throughout their lives.

> —John Calvin, *Institutes of the Christian Religion*, 3.3.9

David R. Nelson, Pastor

Baptist Church of Perry, Perry, NY

Introduction

A confused expression came over the face of a friend when I shared with her the title of this book. "Why *Recovering*?" she asked. Her question—or perhaps challenge—was certainly justified, since *Recovering Repentance* is provocative in that it implies repentance has been lost or forgotten. It's not that I believe the practice of repentance has been totally abandoned, for that would signify the death of the church. Rather, what I am suggesting is that modern Christians have largely lost a biblical and historical *conception* of repentance. This loss has had many grievous effects such as ineffective—or worse, misguided—evangelism, spurious conversions, and the general deterioration of evangelical Christianity.

At the root of this problem is what the late Princeton theologian J. Gresham Machen identified as "a loss of the consciousness of sin." Behaviors that were once classified as sinful are now attributed to illness or victimization, or they are so common that they are simply considered normal. Lacking a sense of sin, many Christian leaders have drastically reinterpreted repentance to make it acceptable to their "righteous" audience. Machen wisely observes:

> The fundamental fault of the modern church is that she is busily engaged in an absolutely impossible task—she is busily engaged in calling the righteous to repentance. Modern preachers are trying to bring men into the Church without requiring them to relinquish their pride; they are trying to help men avoid the conviction of sin.[1]

These teachers may speak of repentance in terms of recovery or deliverance or behavior modification but never brokenness before the holy God whom one has offended.

---

[1] J. Gresham Machen, *Christianity and Liberalism* (New York: MacMillan, 1923), 68.

Other leaders avoid the topic of repentance altogether, considering it irrelevant. They argue that people are constantly bombarded with negative messages and, consequently, need only to hear positive and encouraging messages about God's love and kindness and grace. What they don't realize is that this is only a half-gospel, rooted in a god of their own making. Calling it *Jesus* does not make it God any more than did the Israelites calling the golden calf *Jehovah* (Ex. 32:5).

Further, what these leaders fail to consider is that the journey to eternal life, though commenced in brokenness, ends with eternal wholeness. And although the road is marked with difficulty, it leads to everlasting comfort. But the easy road, which is free of spiritual distress, leads to destruction, even if it is paved with Bibles, lined with churches, and has inspiring messages plastered on its billboards.

Of course, ours is not the first generation with an aversion to repentance. John the Baptist told Herod to repent of his sexual immorality, and was killed for it. Jesus called men to repentance and was crucified. Paul exhorted Felix to repentance and was escorted back to his prison cell. Natural man always has and always will reflexively resist hearing the truth about his condition. As one bold saint has observed: "The man whose little sermon is 'repent' sets himself against his age and will for the time being be battered mercilessly by the age whose moral tone he challenges. There is but one end for such a man—'off with his head!' You had better not try to preach repentance until you have pledged your head to heaven."[2]

Nevertheless, I believe that God is opening the eyes of many and is raising up pastors, teachers, and evangelists who proclaim the full gospel of Jesus Christ, which necessarily includes the exhortation to "repentance toward God and faith toward Jesus Christ" (Acts 20:21). I am much indebted to the saints of past and present who have helped

---

[2] Joseph Parker, quoted in Leonard Ravenhill, *Why Revival Tarries* (Zachary, LA: Fires of Revival, 1972), 95.

me to understand what Scripture teaches about repentance and whose preaching has been the means of God bringing me to experience it.

I gladly acknowledge at the outset that there is nothing novel or original contained herein. Rather, I have aimed to be true to Scripture and in alignment with historic orthodox Christian views on this subject. It is my prayer that those who read this book will gain a deeper understanding of repentance, from which they might go on to experience in a deeper way that spiritual brokenness that leads to wholeness.

Chapter 1

A Biblical View of Repentance

Against You, You only, have I sinned,
And done this evil in Your sight—
That You may be found just when You speak,
And blameless when You judge. (Psalm 51:4)

We might say about the word *repentance* what David exclaimed about Goliath's sword: "There is none like it!" (1 Sam. 21:9). It is unique in its ability to simultaneously convey a disposition of the heart, a frame of mind, a verbal communication, and a course of action. But it is not only a unique word; it is also a sharp word. It implies that there is something fundamentally wrong with us that needs to be changed, that needs to be set right. Unfortunately, its sharp edge has been dulled in our day by the prevailing preference for vagueness and a tendency toward sentimentalism. It is the aim of this chapter to sharpen the blade—to provide a clear definition of repentance that is derived from the Scriptures and consistent with the historic teaching of the church—that we might feel the full force of Jesus's command to "repent and believe in the gospel" (Mark 1:15).

The Meaning of Repentance

In his classic work on Christian orthodoxy, *Mere Christianity*, C. S. Lewis compares the repentant sinner to a rebel laying down his arms, surrendering, willingly humbling himself before and submitting himself to the king he once sought to dethrone.[1] This metaphor is a good starting point from which to unpack the meaning and importance of repentance. As with any metaphor, this one has its limitations, but it provides helpful imagery, so I am going to expand on it a bit.

True repentance is rooted in a right view of God, the King, and an accurate assessment of self, the rebel. In terms of the King, one must see that He is no petty, provincial sovereign but the Maker, Ruler, and Sustainer of all things. Further, he needs to understand some basic facets of the King's nature and character. The first is that the King is supremely righteous—that is, everything He does is good and right. No rebel would willingly subjugate himself to a king whom he suspected of being wicked, for he would neither consider the king superior to himself nor trust the king to deal justly with him upon his surrender. Indeed, the rebel who sees the King's righteousness knows He will do right to him though He put him to death.

Second, the King's purity must be in view—such perfect purity that when the rebel looks upon Him, his own contamination is exposed like a filthy room when the sun's light shines through a window. Such a vision causes him to weep over his own corruption and to seek reconciliation with this Personage.

Furthermore, the rebel will have no delusions of offering the King a gift to appease His anger, for His wrath is not arbitrary or born of wounded pride. Rather, it is the result of a breach of His purity and cannot be quelled unless He freely and sovereignly declares the rebel pure.

Another facet of the King's nature that the rebel must behold is His holiness—that is, that He is set apart from His subjects and totally

---

[1] C. S. Lewis, *Mere Christianity* (New York: Harper Collins, 1952), 59–60.

unlike anything or anyone else in the entire realm over which He reigns. This instills in the rebel's heart a healthy fear of the King and shows him that the King cannot be approached on any terms other than those that He Himself sets forth.

In terms of self, before one will lay down his arms, he must first acknowledge that he is actually in rebellion and that, in light of whom he is rebelling against, his actions are both wrong and foolish. If he thinks that his treasonous actions are simply the product of bad genes, illness, or a hard childhood, he will not apprehend the severity of his situation. Neither will he recognize his need to surrender if he considers his offenses to be primarily against his fellow citizens, for they are his equals. And why should he humble himself before them? Finally, he must be brought to prize reconciliation with the King more highly than remaining in defiance against Him. As long as rebellion ranks higher on his list of values than peace with the King, he will not lay down his arms.

Hopefully some will find Lewis's metaphor (and my expansion of it) helpful in understanding the essence of repentance. But a metaphor is only good if it conveys a true proposition. And for the Christian, the standard of truth is God's written word. Therefore, we'll examine what Scripture reveals concerning the meaning and importance of repentance.

Repentance is an important theme throughout the Bible. In both Hebrew (*shuv*) and Greek (*metanoeo*), the words translated *repentance* signify a change of heart, mind, and purpose. Let's flesh out this definition by looking at specific examples from both the Old and New Testaments that illustrate what repentance is and is not.

What Repentance Is Not

It may be helpful initially to think about what repentance is not or, more accurately, what it does not solely consist of. In doing this, we'll examine the account in Mark 5 in which Jesus encounters a multi-demonic entity named Legion who had taken up residence in a man living in the country of the Gadarenes. For if there are aspects of repentance that a demon can display—and we know that demons cannot repent—we can therefore conclude that these aspects must not constitute the whole of repentance.

> Then they came to the other side of the sea, to the country of the Gadarenes. And when He had come out of the boat, immediately there met Him out of the tombs a man with an unclean spirit, who had his dwelling among the tombs; and no one could bind him, not even with chains, because he had often been bound with shackles and chains. And the chains had been pulled apart by him, and the shackles broken in pieces; neither could anyone tame him. And always, night and day, he was in the mountains and in the tombs, crying out and cutting himself with stones.
>
> When he saw Jesus from afar, he ran and worshiped Him. And he cried out with a loud voice and said, "What have I to do with You, Jesus, Son of the Most High God? I implore You by God that You do not torment me."
>
> For He said to him, "Come out of the man, unclean spirit!" Then He asked him, "What is your name?"
>
> And he answered, saying, "My name is Legion; for we are many." Also he begged Him earnestly that He would not send them out of the country. (Mark 5:1–10)

First, the demon recognizes and admits, albeit tacitly, that he is morally depraved. This can be observed in several parts of the passage. The word *unclean* refers to moral impurity and corruption, and when Jesus identifies him as an "unclean spirit," the demon does not dispute this fact. Demons know they are evil—and they love it. This demon knows he is utterly wicked and corrupt and that Jesus is completely righteous. He therefore asks Jesus, "What have I to do with You?" The obvious answer is *nothing*, for light shares nothing in common with darkness, and righteousness has nothing to do with unrighteousness (2 Cor. 6:14).

If demons recognize and admit their own wickedness, then this must indicate human beings may do as much without necessarily being the object of the Holy Spirit's working. Indeed, the apostle Paul tells us in Romans 1:32 that wicked men know their actions are evil and God's judgment is against them, but they do them anyway.

Another thing we learn from Jesus's interaction with the demon is that repentance is not simply begging God for mercy. The demon does as much when he asks Jesus not to send him back to hell but instead allow him to enter a nearby herd of pigs. Legion apparently knew what hell was like and did not want to be sent there. So it was out of self-preservation and desire to avoid suffering that he asked Jesus to have mercy on him.

Similarly, people, if they have a right conception of hell, desire to avoid it for fear of the suffering they will experience there. They may hear a sermon on hellfire preached from the pulpit, be driven to confess every sin they've ever committed, and say the "Sinner's Prayer" ten times just for good measure. But while fear may be a starting point that leads us to repentance, if it ends there it is not repentance in the biblical sense. As the Puritan Thomas Watson put it: "If pain and trouble were sufficient for repentance, then the damned in hell would be the most penitent, for they are most in anguish. Repentance depends upon a change of heart. There may be terror and yet no change of heart."[2]

Undoubtedly, the demon did not believe he was actually repenting. This example does not illustrate false repentance but merely shows attitudes that in themselves could not possibly constitute repentance.

---

[2] Thomas Watson, *The Doctrine of Repentance* (Carlisle: Banner of Truth, 2011), 6.

False Repentance

Now let's examine a case in Scripture that illustrates false repentance, so that we might further define it negatively—that is, to gain a better understanding of what it is by seeing clearly what it's not.

The first example is seen in the life (and death) of Judas Iscariot. In Matthew 27:3–5 we are told concerning him: "Then Judas, His betrayer, seeing that He had been condemned, was remorseful and brought back the thirty pieces of silver to the chief priests and elders, saying, 'I have sinned by betraying innocent blood.' And they said, 'What is that to us? You see to it!' Then he threw down the pieces of silver in the temple and departed, and went and hanged himself.

Let's look at three facets of false repentance in this passage.

First, "Judas . . . was remorseful." Judas was sorry for what he had done. Despite being a wicked man and a virtual puppet of Satan, he was still a man. And every man retains a faint glimmer of the image of God that was stamped on Adam and corrupted by the fall. So, because of his corrupted nature, Judas had simultaneously in his heart both an affinity for evil—making him available for Satan's use—and an aversion to it because of the remaining traces of God's image. Up until the point when Judas realized what he had done, Satan blinded him spiritually and prevented him from appreciating the evil of his betrayal of Christ. But at the point of his realization, God allowed his eyes to be opened and his natural revulsion of betrayal to kick in.

Of course, this was not your average treachery but the handing over for execution the only innocent man who had ever lived. So, the depth of Judas's sorrow corresponded to the hideousness of the evil he had committed. But it is important to note this was at the *natural* level; there was no infusion of God's grace into his soul that brought him to remorse. The apostle Paul draws a distinction in 2 Corinthians 7:10 between godly sorrow (to be explored in the next section), which produces repentance, and worldly sorrow, which leads only to death.

Judas clearly experienced worldly, or natural, sorrow, which is of no spiritual value. It is the same kind of sorrow we might feel if we were to lose our fortune or be diagnosed with a terminal illness. Both are obviously negative events, and the God-given desire for self-preservation does not allow us to be ambivalent when struck by these tragedies. But the resulting sorrow we feel is merely an indication that we are normal human beings; it is therefore natural, or worldly. It leads to death because it does not in itself change the spiritual path on which a person is walking. Thus, being sorry over sin is not necessarily an indication of genuine repentance.

Second, Judas admits, "I have sinned by betraying innocent blood." The next act of Judas's pseudo-repentance is his confession of sin. If we didn't know how Judas's story ends, we might be convinced by his confession that he was truly penitent. Confession of sin is most certainly one aspect of genuine repentance, so this seems to be in his favor. But we know that Judas is presently in hell, so his repentance was obviously false.

Does the Holy Spirit provide any clues as to the deficiency of Judas's confession? I believe He does. First, his confession was the product of the terror over his impending destruction and the worldly sorrow that were welling up within him. If the spring is polluted, then the streams that flow from it will also be polluted. In other words, his confession was corrupt because it was rooted in self-preservation and servile fear. Second, Judas confessed his sin not to God but to man. Scripture makes it clear that all sin is committed against God alone (Ps. 51:4), for He is the One whose law has been violated. And if all sin is against God, how much more this one, which was against the Son Himself.

Yet Judas did not confess that he betrayed the Son of God or the Messiah or even a prophet for that matter, only that he had betrayed "innocent blood." Perhaps this was simply because he never acknowledged, much less believed, that Jesus was any of those. However, it is also possible that he would have given intellectual assent to Jesus's divine identity, but even in his confession he was trying to downplay his sin by referring to Him only as an innocent man. Moreover, since Judas had sinned against God alone, only God could forgive him; the priests to whom he confessed could not—and would not—offer him any comfort.

Third, "Judas . . . brought back the thirty pieces of silver to the chief priests and elders." In a desperate effort to unburden his guilt-laden conscience, Judas returned the money he had been paid to betray Jesus. In effect, he was trying to undo his evil deed, to right the wrong, to turn back the clock. One might even say he was turning away from his sin. But the nature of his sin meant it could not be undone or somehow stopped. This act of repentance was false and futile, intended only to relieve his remorse.

From this we learn that discontinuing a particular sin is not necessarily a sign of genuine repentance, for it may stem from worldly sorrow, self-love, or fear. If this is the case, it will inevitably be exchanged for other sins. It is said that nature abhors a vacuum; so does the human soul. This is why Jesus said that when an unclean spirit leaves a man for a while and then returns to find his soul neat and well-kept, he will go and find seven other spirits and bring them back with him to dwell in the man's soul (Matt. 12:42–45).

To illustrate this point, let's say that a woman is leading a sexually promiscuous life. Then one day it occurs to her that she is jeopardizing her health by living that way. Moreover, she has been feeling guilty about her behavior since she started going to church. So she forsakes that lifestyle altogether, settles down, gets married, and becomes a member of her church. Now she is puffed up with pride because she was able to drag herself out of the gutter and find a better way to live. Not only that, she begins to look with contempt at women who remain trapped in her former lifestyle. "Why don't they see that they are destroying their lives?" she wonders with self-righteous frustration. "They need to get their act together like I did." The woman simply traded one sin for two others, equally grievous and offensive in the sight of God.

And so it goes with all those who have discontinued a sin but have not truly repented. They are like the gardener who breaks off a weed at the base but does not pull out the root. The weed then grows back with four or five stems, even more deeply rooted than it initially was. Charles Spurgeon likewise warns against this type of repentance: "Let none of us fancy that we have repented when we have only a false and fictitious repentance; let none of us take that to be the work of the Spirit which is only the work of poor human nature; let us not dream that we have savingly turned to God, when, perhaps, we have only turned to ourselves. And let us not think it enough to have turned from one vice to another, or from vice to virtue."[3]

As it turns out, "poor human nature" is capable of more than most people think. By a sheer act of the will, a person has the power to break addictions, resist powerful temptations, reform his life, and perform spectacular feats. And this power is amplified by religious experience. Nineteenth-century Harvard psychologist William James provides numerous illustrations of this in his classic work, *The Varieties of Religious Experience*. In one case, a forty-year-old woman who had been plagued with sickness and depression her entire life experienced a profound "conversion" to pantheism and subsequent healing and inner transformation.[4] This is just one of the many examples that James provides of the power of the psyche. Clearly, human nature is capable of a great deal. It does not, however, have the ability to liberate itself from bondage to sin; the cruel master will subjugate his slave in one way or another unless a more powerful master redeems him.

---

[3] "Turn or Burn," Sermon No. 106, *The Spurgeon Center*, accessed December 21, 2017, https://www.spurgeon.org/resource-library/sermons.

[4] William James, *The Varieties of Religious Experience* (New York: Random House, 1929), 102–103.

To summarize, we have negatively defined repentance by examining what it is not—specifically, merely recognizing that one is hell-bound, a certain kind of admitting or confessing of one's sins, begging God for mercy out of fear and self-love, being remorseful with worldly sorrow, and even turning away from particular sins.

Discernment vs. Judgment

I want to issue a word of caution before we proceed. We can look at Judas in retrospect and say with certainty that his repentance was spurious, not only because there are indications in the act itself but because we are told unequivocally that he was lost (John 17:12). In addition, we do not see any evidence afterward that he had genuinely repented. In fact, we see compelling evidence to the contrary— namely, his suicide. But we ought to be exceedingly careful when trying to determine whether someone else has repented, as we see only the surface and cannot see into the heart. We can certainly search for signs one way or the other, especially when the person is a candidate for the ministry or if we are considering entering into an important partnership with him or her (e.g., marriage, deep friendship, business partnership). Indeed, Jesus said that we will know them by the fruit they produce. If we do not see fruits of repentance, it would be dangerous to partner in any significant way with that person. In the end though, God alone knows the heart, and He will judge righteously.

Therefore, we must always be wary of the tendency of our fallen nature to judge others in a condemnatory manner, especially in light of James 4:11–12. In this passage, James warns us that the person who judges his brother judges the law and is therefore "not a doer of the law but a judge" (v. 11). In other words, the person who judges his brother does so from a position of self-exaltation in his own heart and mind. Not only has he elevated himself over his brother in order to judge him but he has also put himself in the very place of God, who gave the law and "is able to save and to destroy" (v. 12) according to

His perfect justice. The man who judges another is in a dangerous position and must himself repent of his pride.

What then should the Christian do who sees little evidence of the grace of repentance in the life of a professing believer? If that person is living in open sin, then church discipline is in order, and the principles given in Matthew 18 and 1 Corinthians 5 should be carried out. Even then, we are commanded to "not count him as an enemy, but admonish him as a brother" (2 Thess. 3:15). But if (as is more often the case) the person simply seems to be struggling with a certain sin and lacking "fruits worthy of repentance" (Luke 3:8), then I believe that 1 John 5:16 applies, which tells us to pray for our brother who sins. If we love our brother out of love for God—that is, we desire his deliverance for the sake of the glory of God's grace and power being displayed—then we will pray with fervency, and even tears, to that end.

What Repentance Is

Next we'll begin to positively define repentance by examining passages of Scripture that speak of it either directly or indirectly. I have found helpful the way in which Puritan Thomas Watson divides repentance into six parts: sight of sin, sorrow for sin, hatred of sin, shame for sin, confession of sin, and turning from sin.

Sight of Sin

The first part of repentance is seeing sin—that is, awareness and acknowledgment of it. It is illustrated at the point in the parable of the prodigal son where "[the prodigal] came to himself" and concluded that he ought to return home and confess his sin to his father (Luke 15:17–18). And it is that to which Solomon referred when he spoke of each man seeing "the plague of his own heart" (1 Kings 8:38). The plague of leprosy is an especially fitting metaphor for sin because it is a disease that causes nerve damage, leaving its victim unable to feel pain. In like manner, sin gradually eats away at

11

one's moral nerve so that he can no longer feel the sting of conscience. Sin sears the conscience like a hot iron, Paul tells us in 1 Timothy 4:2. And Satan blinds men's minds (2 Cor. 4:4), making them unable to see their sin. In Watson's characteristically poignant words: "Persons are veiled-over with ignorance and self-love; therefore they do not see what deformed souls they have. The devil does with them as the falconer does with the hawk. He blinds them and carries them hooded to hell."[5]

However, it may be more accurate to say that this aspect of repentance is seeing God and then seeing oneself in the light of God's perfect righteousness, purity, and holiness. There are no instances in Scripture of a person coming to accurately see his sin without first encountering God. For example, after God finished speaking to him, Job said, "I have heard of You by the hearing of the ear, but now my eye sees You. Therefore I abhor myself, and repent in dust and ashes" (Job 42:5–6). Similarly, Peter, in Luke 5:8, after following Jesus's instructions concerning where to put down his fishing net and subsequently catching literal boatloads of fish, realized who Jesus was and cried out, "Depart from me, for I am a sinful man, O Lord!" Again, it was when Isaiah the prophet stood in the presence of God and saw Him that he exclaimed, "Woe is me, for I am undone! Because I am a man of unclean lips . . . For my eyes have seen the King, The LORD of hosts" (Isa. 6:5).

This includes not only the sight of one's particular sins but also of his sinful nature, for a person cannot repent unless he sees both his sin and his sinfulness. He is not a sinner because he commits sin; rather, he commits sin because he is a sinner. Who a person is determines what he does. In philosophical terms, essence precedes existence. And to be able to repent, one must see these two aspects of his sin. Therefore, the person who merely concedes, "I've done some bad

---

[5] Watson, *Repentance*, 8.

things in my life," even confessing the things he has done, does not have an accurate view of his sin.

Psalm 51 illustrates well the view of sin that is part of true repentance. It is a song that King David penned after his affair with Bathsheba and ensuing murder of her husband, Uriah. He writes, "I acknowledge my transgressions" (v. 3); this refers to his particular sins. Then in verse 5 he demonstrates understanding of the inherent corruption that is the root of his sinful acts: "Behold, I was brought forth in iniquity, and in sin my mother conceived me."

Concerning this element of repentance, the eminent eighteenth-century evangelist George Whitefield said in his sermon "The Method of Grace":

> Before ever, therefore, you can speak peace to your hearts, conviction must go deeper; you must not only be convinced of your actual transgressions against the law of God, but likewise of the foundation of all your transgressions. And what is that? I mean original sin, that original corruption each of us brings into the world with us, which renders us liable to God's wrath and damnation. . . . There is pride, malice, and revenge, in all our hearts; and this temper cannot come from God; it comes from our first parent, Adam, who, after he fell from God, fell out of God into the devil.[6]

Sorrow for Sin

Genuine repentance must begin with the sight of sin, but it will not end there. The next piece of repentance is sorrow for sin. In 2 Corinthians 7:10, the apostle Paul refers to the kind of sorrow that the penitent soul experiences. The NKJV translates it as "godly sorrow" that "produces repentance." But a more literal translation renders it "sorrow toward God" that "works repentance" (YLT). This is a

---

[6] Christian Classics Ethereal Library, "The Method of Grace," accessed December 21, 2017, www.ccel.org/ccel/whitefield/sermons.lx.html.

relatively minor point, but it may help us to gain deeper insight into the meaning of Paul's words. The NKJV translation might be taken to mean that godly sorrow is distinct from repentance—that is, if it "produces" repentance then it cannot be part of it, making repentance something else. But to say that it "works" repentance can be understood to mean that it *performs* it (as it does in Rom. 7:18). Or, to put it another way, Paul is not saying godly sorrow births repentance as a woman births an infant but that it carries it out, brings it to pass, executes it, like the labor process causes the delivery of the baby. Godly sorrow and repentance are always linked; one will not be seen without the other.

Further support for this interpretation comes from the second half of the verse, which states: "But the sorrow of the world produces [same Greek word] death." So worldly sorrow working death is contrasted with godly sorrow working repentance. We know that death is not simply a future event, but for the unregenerate, it is a present state of being (1 Tim. 5:6). Therefore, the unbeliever, as long as he practices worldly sorrow in lieu of godly sorrow, is continually bringing forth death within himself until the culmination of this process in the day he is cast into the lake of fire (Rev. 20:14). This suggests that while godly sorrow is not the entirety of repentance—or even synonymous with it—it is an essential aspect of it. This is why Paul says in the preceding verse (v. 9) that he is exceedingly glad the Corinthian believers were sad with godly sorrow when they saw they were offending God by welcoming immorality into their church.

King David was no stranger to godly sorrow. Psalms 6, 32, 38, 51, 102, 130, and 143 are known as the Penitential Psalms of David and are of great assistance to us as we seek to define repentance and get a sense of the inner anguish that is an essential part of it. These psalms show us that he not only saw his sin but that his heart was broken over it.

14

Here are a few examples:

- "I am weary with my groaning; All night I make my bed swim; I drench my couch with my tears" (Ps. 6:6).

- "For I will declare my iniquity; I will be in anguish over my sin" (Ps. 38:18).

- "For I have eaten ashes like bread, and mingled my drink with weeping" (Ps. 102:9).

It is important to understand that David was not upset because he had been caught in his sin or because of the punishment he received. He rightly viewed those consequences as God's discipline, and he knew that God disciplines those whom He loves to keep their souls from destruction. Rather, David's tears flowed from a heart that was aligned with the heart of God. He was called a man after God's heart, which was not an attestation that he was without sin or even that he found no pleasure in sin. It was rooted in the fact that when he saw his sin, it was grievous to him. He saw it was a violation of the person and the commandment of the infinitely good God, and that caused him great anguish of soul.

Furthermore, in verses 16-17 of Psalm 51 David writes, "For You do not desire sacrifice, or else I would give it; You do not delight in burnt offering. The sacrifices of God are a broken spirit, a broken and a contrite heart—These, O God, You will not despise."

To fully appreciate what David is saying here, we must understand that the ceremonial law God gave to Israel on Mount Sinai established a system of sacrifices and offerings by which people's sins might be covered. Within this system, if an individual sinned, he could bring a young goat to the priest, who would then kill the goat and sprinkle its blood on the altar. It was assumed that the man who sinned would feel the gravity and horror of his sin as the innocent animal's blood was shed instead of his own. But over time, authentic religious practice gave way to externalism—as it often does—and people developed a casual attitude toward sin. Many would simply fulfill their religious duty by bringing their sacrifice to the priest and then put the whole ordeal behind them.

However, David understood the essence of the sacrificial system. He perceived that God's requisites for covering sin could not be fulfilled by simply going through the prescribed process of killing an animal. In fact, he went so far as to say that God is not satisfied with sacrifices and offerings—rather, He delights in the sinner's brokenness over his sin. This was God's original intent in giving the sacrificial system, and this alone is acceptable to Him.

Another example of godly sorrow is seen in Jesus's parable in Luke 18. In this story, a tax collector (whom Jesus's hearers would have considered to be the dregs of Jewish society and virtually without hope of salvation) goes to the temple to pray. He brings no sacrifice to offer for his sins, nor does he even encounter a priest. His only actions are to lower his head, indicating utter shame, and to beat his chest, showing profound grief. He speaks no eloquent prayers; indeed, his petition consists of only seven words: "God, be merciful to me a sinner!" (v. 13). And Jesus states unequivocally that this man went home justified—that is, righteous in the sight of God, saved. In saying this, Jesus proclaims that the publican's sorrow was sincere and his repentance of the saving kind.

However, we must be cautious of the bent toward externalism that plagues human nature. Some well-meaning interpreters might attempt to create from this passage a formula for repentance, but no such formula exists. Another person might say and do the same things as the publican but go home no better off than when he came. Conversely, one might be filled with godly sorrow but express it in a way completely different from that of the man in this passage. Jesus is not instructing us how to repent, or how to be saved for that matter. He is indicating the kind of person who is truly repentant and is being saved. The publican's words and deeds were an outward manifestation of what he was experiencing in his soul. Thus, they were not the cause of his justification but were visible signs of the grace of God and the operation of the Holy Spirit.

Hatred of Sin

The next aspect of repentance is likewise a passion of the soul—namely, hatred of sin. To hate sin is to be disgusted by it as sincerely as one is repulsed when he sees the decaying flesh of a leper. This is why Solomon aptly used leprosy as a metaphor for sin in his prayer recorded in 1 Kings 8:38. He prayed that God would hear the plea for mercy of the man who knows "the plague of his own heart."

An anecdote from the late British journalist Malcolm Muggeridge will serve to illustrate this concept. He was living in India, teaching journalism, thousands of miles from his wife and children. One day he decided to go for a swim in the Ganges River and noticed a woman bathing in the distance. He was consumed with lust, and he knew that nothing would stop him from fulfilling his desire. So he began to swim out to her. As he drew near, he paused, looked up, and was horrified by what he saw: a woman whose body had been ravaged by leprosy. Her nose was partially eaten away, and oozing white blotches covered her skin. He was initially filled with revulsion at the sight of this woman until he realized that the corruption of her body paled in comparison to the corruption of his adulterous heart.[7] So it is with all who experience the profound hatred for sin that is a vital part of repentance.

One instance of this in Scripture is found in the book of Job. As far as (mere) men go, Job was among the most righteous that have ever lived (1:1), and he knew it. Throughout his season of suffering he

---

[7] Richard D. Phillips, *What's So Great about the Doctrines of Grace?* (Sanford, FL: Reformation Trust, 2008), 17.

clung to the notion that he had done nothing to deserve the calamity that God had brought upon him: "I put on righteousness, and it clothed me; My justice was like a robe and a turban" (29:14). But at the end of the book, when God spoke to him out of the whirlwind, He made no apologies to Job. The Lord simply reminded him that He was the One who created the heavens and the earth and sovereignly exercises His authority and dominion over creation as He sees fit. By the end of God's discourse, Job recognized he wasn't as righteous as he had supposed, and God was much more righteous and powerful than he had imagined, and he cried out, "Therefore I abhor myself, and repent in dust and ashes" (42:6).

Job's hatred for himself was born out of the realization of how sinful he truly was. In the realm of men, he was a moral giant, but in the eyes of God, he was a soul marred by sin. He tasted for himself the bitter poison of sin that had coursed through the veins of man since the fall, and in that moment everything about himself he once considered good and sweet became utterly nauseating and hateful. Or, in the words of Solomon, Job saw the plague of his own heart. And as Thomas Watson rightly states, "We are never more precious in God's eyes than when we are lepers in our own."[8]

Spurgeon attests to the importance of hatred for sin when he says:

> When a man repents with that grace of repentance which God the Spirit works in him, he repents not of the punishment which is to follow the deed, but of the deed itself; and he feels that if there were not a pit digged for the wicked, if there were no ever-gnawing worm, and no fire unquenchable, he would still hate sin. It is such repentance as this which every one of you must have, or else you will be lost. It must be a hatred of sin. Do not suppose, that because when you come to die you will be afraid of eternal torment, therefore that will be repentance. Every thief is afraid of

---

[8] Watson, *Repentance*, 45.

the prison; but he will steal to-morrow if you set him free. Most men who have committed murder tremble at the sight of the gallows-tree, but they would do the deed again could they live. It is not the hatred of the punishment that is repentance; it is the hatred of the deed itself.[9]

It is impossible for someone to repent who loves his sin, whether it be the open and outright love of the hedonist or the secret, hidden love of the religious Pharisee. The lover of pleasure does not care about the nature of sin or its consequences, so long as he experiences the pleasure that they afford. In his mind, sin is relative; he's not as bad as other people he knows. And hell is either an old wives' tale, on par with Santa Claus and meant to keep children in line, or it is a much more enjoyable place than heaven. At any rate, it's a small price to pay for a lifetime of pleasure, so he reasons.

The Pharisee, on the other hand, is averse to the effects of sin, like the social stigma and the prospect of eternal punishment, that accompany it. So he becomes a legalist, ever interested in how much he can do without "crossing the line" and overtly sinning. He prides himself on his obedience of the command, on his moral rectitude, but is blind to the fact that he is inwardly "full of dead men's bones and all uncleanness" (Matt. 23:27). It's not that he doesn't see his sin; he does, but it doesn't disturb him much. What does cause him distress, however, is the fear of punishment that might come from it—he fears the loss of what he loves, he fears consequences, he fears hell. He prays that God will forgive him and help him not to sin, and he does his best to suppress the wicked, lustful, perverse thoughts that fill his mind. Nevertheless, he does these not because he hates his sin but because he fears what will come of it.

This is not to say that the person who has truly repented will never again sin. For as long as he is in this mortal body, he will wrestle

---

[9] Spurgeon, "Turn or Burn."

against sin. But he *will* fight it, not because of fear but because of hatred. He says, along with Paul, "For what I am doing, I do not understand. For what I will to do, that I do not practice; but what I hate, that I do. . . . O wretched man that I am! Who will deliver me from this body of death?" (Rom. 7:15, 24). Paul never made peace with his sin but hated it more and more as he daily became more like Christ. And like Paul (to greater or lesser degrees), those who are penitent will sincerely, objectively hate their sin.

In *The Pilgrim's Progress*, a man named Talkative joins Christian and Faithful on their journey to the Celestial City. Faithful, though initially encouraged by Talkative's eagerness to discuss spiritual things, comes to question his authenticity. He tests Talkative by asking him how the grace of God is manifested in a person's heart. Talkative responds that grace shows itself by causing a "great outcry against sin," and he is about to go on to his second point when Faithful interrupts him to point out his error. Rather than causing a man to cry out against sin, Faithful explains, grace stirs up hatred for sin in his heart. When Talkative asks what the difference is, Faithful replies:

> Oh, a great deal. A man may cry out against sin of policy, but he cannot abhor it, but by virtue of a godly antipathy against it. I have heard many cry out against sin in the pulpit, who yet can abide it well enough in the heart, house, and conversation. Joseph's mistress cried out with a loud voice, as if she had been very holy; but she would willingly, notwithstanding that, have committed uncleanness with him.[10]

Shame for Sin

The fourth aspect of repentance is shame for sin. The penitent sinner realizes that he was created, in the words of the Westminster Catechism, to glorify God and enjoy Him forever. But he sees that he

---

[10] John Bunyan, *The Pilgrim's Progress* (New York: Barnes & Noble, 2005), 95.

has strayed far from that purpose, and he is ashamed at this realization. His sin begins to make him blush. Like Adam, he sees that he is naked, exposed, without any covering. Watson describes this kind of shame as "a holy bashfulness."[11] When Ezra the priest was informed that the Jews had taken wives from the pagan peoples around them, he cried out to God, "I am ashamed and blush to lift up my face to thee, my God: for our iniquities are increased over our head, and our trespass is grown up unto the heavens" (Ezra 9:6 KJV). In Jesus's parable, the prodigal was so ashamed of his waywardness that he expected upon returning home to be treated not like a son but a servant (Luke 15:20). Similarly, in the parable of the penitent publican, we saw that this man "would not even raise his eyes to heaven," out of shame for his sin (Luke 18:13).

In stark contrast to these examples of holy shame are those who have lost their ability to blush. They are ashamed of nothing; indeed, they are often proud of their sin. They are the ones of whom Paul says "[their] glory is in their shame" (Phil. 3:19). They boast of their immorality—like the men described by the prophet Isaiah who brag about their ability to hold their liquor (Isa. 5:22) and the adulterous woman in Proverbs who "wipes her mouth, and says, 'I have done no wickedness'" (Prov. 30:20).

Those who do not experience shame in life will most certainly experience it after they die. They will be like the guest in the parable of the wedding feast, who is found to not have the proper wedding garment and is consequently thrown into outer darkness (Matt. 22:12-13). If he had experienced the shame beforehand of acknowledging he didn't have the appropriate attire and requested that it be given to him, he would have avoided the ultimate shame of being thrown out of the feast. Likewise, those who embrace the shame

---

[11] Watson, *Repentance*, 39.

of repentance now can rest assured they will not be put to shame when Christ appears in His glory (1 Peter 2:6; Rev. 3:18).

Confession of Sin

The next facet of repentance, confession of sin, proceeds naturally from, and is totally dependent on, the first four. If a person has seen his sin for what it is, grieved over it, hated it, and been ashamed of it, he will naturally feel compelled to confess it. It is self-recrimination, a verbal indictment against self, demonstrating one's knowledge of his own wickedness. He makes no attempt to justify sin with reasons and excuses but takes full responsibility. Further, it is a sincere acknowledgment that one does not deserve the forgiveness and favor of the offended party (which is always God). The thief on the cross next to Jesus confessed, "And we indeed justly [are condemned], for we receive the due reward of our deeds" (Luke 23:41). The Holy Spirit unequivocally affirms (through the apostle John) that confession is an essential part of repentance: "If we confess our sins, He is faithful and just to forgive us our sins and to cleanse us from all unrighteousness" (1 John 1:9).

Consider again the prodigal son. Upon returning to his father he confessed, "Father, I have sinned against heaven and in your sight, and am no longer worthy to be called your son" (Luke 15:21). Notice there is no ambiguity about whom the son's sin is against (namely, God) and that it was committed in the sight of his father. This is no minor detail. We must understand that all sin is against God, because He is the One whose command has been broken and whose standard has been violated. Therefore, while it is generally right to confess our sin to the person or people it affected and to issue a heartfelt apology, confession as it relates to repentance is toward God alone.

This is the reason, according to the model prayer given by Jesus, we are to pray, "Forgive us our sins, for we also forgive everyone who is indebted to us" (Luke 11:4). We may be indebted to one another for the way we have acted toward each other, and we can confess and offer forgiveness on the horizontal level, but it is God who forgives our sins, for they are against Him. This truth is affirmed when Nathan the prophet confronts David concerning his sin with Bathsheba, saying, "Why have you despised the commandment of the LORD, to do evil in His sight? You have killed Uriah the Hittite with the sword; you have taken his wife to be your wife, and have killed him with the sword of the people of Ammon" (2 Sam. 12:9). David responds, "I have sinned against the LORD" (v. 13). Moreover, in his psalm of repentance, David confesses: "Against You, You only, have I sinned, and done this evil in Your sight" (Ps. 51:4). In both Nathan's indictment and David's confession, God is the focal point, for He was the One offended by David's sin.

Confession that is part of genuine repentance cannot be institutionalized or externally compelled. For when a person confesses his sin out of obligation or compulsion, it is necessarily inauthentic; it does not flow from a changed heart and mind but from self-love or self-preservation. Rather, confession must be a sort of free and voluntary venting of a heart that has seen, and been troubled by, its own corruption.

The Fruit of Repentance

The final aspect of true repentance is turning from sin. This might more accurately be identified as the fruit of repentance rather than a part of repentance itself. Nevertheless, it is so closely associated with repentance in Scripture that it seems wise to include it in this section. Turning from sin and doing "works befitting repentance" (Acts 26:20) are the evidence that a person's sight of sin, sorrow for sin, hatred for sin, shame for sin, and confession of sin were all genuine. For if he seems to demonstrate all these and yet continues to practice the same sin, it would be reasonable (not to mention, biblically warranted) to conclude that he has not truly repented.

In chapter 3 of Luke's Gospel, we are told that many came to receive from John the "baptism of repentance" (v. 3). Baptism had previously been a ceremony reserved for those Gentiles who wanted to convert to Judaism, who wanted to be part of Jehovah's covenant people. So, the fact that many ethnic Jews came to John to be baptized indicates they knew their hearts were far from God and they needed to be reconciled to Him, to be converted. This seemed to show a remarkable change of heart on their part—genuine repentance—but John nevertheless exhorted them to "bear fruits worthy of repentance" (v. 8). In other words, he was telling them to live their lives in a way that corresponded to their purported change of heart. And he warned them that if they fell once again into the spiritually complacent mindset of thinking they were in right standing with God simply because they were Abraham's offspring, they would be putting themselves in grave danger, as "every tree which does not bear good fruit is cut down and thrown into the fire" (v. 9). For in so doing, they would be showing that their repentance was superficial and altogether worthless.

Notice the questions John's listeners asked and how he answered them concerning the fruit of repentance:

> So the people asked him, saying, "What shall we do then?"
>
> He answered and said to them, "He who has two tunics, let him give to him who has none; and he who has food, let him do likewise."
>
> Then tax collectors also came to be baptized, and said to him, "Teacher, what shall we do?"
>
> And he said to them, "Collect no more than what is appointed for you."
>
> Likewise the soldiers asked him, saying, "And what shall we do?"

So he said to them, "Do not intimidate anyone or accuse falsely, and be content with your wages." (vv. 10–14)

Each of these changes of action commanded by John is the natural outworking of a profound change of heart. The giving of extra food and clothing to those in need signifies a decisive break with the sins of covetousness and selfishness. For the tax collectors (who tended to supplement their wages by telling the taxpayer he owed more than he actually did, pocketing the extra), it represented a break from the sins of greed and dishonesty. To the soldiers, John's exhortation to gentleness and contentment spoke to the outward manifestation of their repentance from violence and covetousness. Again, John was not saying, "Repent by doing these things," but "If you have experienced true repentance in your heart, here are the ways in which you need to work it out."

Clearly, the evidence or fruit of genuine repentance is to turn from one's sins to God, which is manifested in a visibly changed life. There are countless examples of this in Scripture, but for our purposes, one will suffice: Saul of Tarsus, who became Paul the apostle. Saul had been a zealous defender of the Jewish faith and a member of the strictest sect of Jews, the Pharisees. He took great pride in his persecution of Christians, even approving the brutal murder of Stephen, the first Christian martyr (Acts 8:1).

It was to this end that Saul, "still breathing threats and murder against the disciples of the Lord" (Acts 9:1), set out for Damascus. But on his way, he encountered the living Christ, repented, and was forever changed. He became even more zealous for the name of Christ than he had been against it. Instead of persecuting Christians, he loved and supported them. And he spent the rest of his life spreading the message he had once sought to destroy. Paul renounced his old way of life and never went back to it. To be sure, he still sinned after his conversion, but he was never again ruled by sin. He had a new master—Jesus Christ. The fruits of Paul's repentance were abundant and lasting, and so will they be of all who have experienced genuine repentance.

Vertical Reconciliation

One final aspect of the fruit of repentance is making restitution—making amends for the wrong committed. There are several places in the law that deal with this topic, one of which is found in Numbers 5:5–7, when the Lord tells Moses, "Speak to the children of Israel: 'When a man or woman commits any sin that men commit in unfaithfulness against the LORD, and that person is guilty, then he shall confess the sin which he has committed. He shall make restitution for his trespass in full, plus one-fifth of it, and give it to the one he has wronged.'"

So, if someone had sinned against God by stealing or otherwise depriving another of that which God had given them, he was to confess his sin and then repay the victim the original amount plus an additional 20 percent. The concept being conveyed is that horizontal (interpersonal) reconciliation is often an important part of vertical (divine) reconciliation. This is further evidenced in Christ's statement that if a man wants to bring a gift to the temple but then remembers that his brother is holding something against him, he must go and reconcile with his brother and then offer the gift to God (Matt. 5:23–24). We also observe this principle in Luke 19 when Zacchaeus, a tax collector, heard Christ's call, and his first impulse was to restore fourfold to those he had defrauded.

However, there are instances where restitution is impossible—for example, when the victim has died and therefore cannot be repaid. God instructed Moses that in this situation, the person should restore the money to the person's relative. If there was no living relative, then he was to bring the money, along with a ram, to the priest, and the priest would make atonement for him (Num. 5:8).

It is worth noting that there were no instructions for reconciliation in the case of sins like murder, adultery, and Sabbath-breaking. These were capital offenses that were punishable by stoning. How then, we might ask, should someone make restitution who has committed one of these sins (i.e., sins for which making restitution is impossible) in modern times? If it is a sin dealt with by the penal code of one's nation, then he ought to subject himself to the penalty prescribed by law. One recent example of this can be seen in the case of a young man who had been sexually abusing his younger sister for a decade. One Sunday morning he went to church, heard the gospel, and repented and believed. He confessed his sin to one of the pastors, who advised him to turn himself in to the authorities. He is now serving time in prison according to the law. Clearly, there is nothing he can ever do to make restitution to his sister, but his actions have thus far been consistent with true repentance.

There may also be occasions in which a person commits a grievous sin for which there is no penalty prescribed by law. I know a dear Christian brother who, before coming to Christ, convinced his girlfriend to murder their unborn child. While he has repented of this sin, he has no means of making restitution nor legal consequences to which he can subject himself. He can only experience vertical reconciliation. The sole course of action available to him is to trust in the "ram of the atonement" prescribed in the law—the one typified by the ram that God provided Abraham in the place of his son Isaac (Gen. 22:13).

As we have seen, repentance is at its core a change of mind whereby a person is brought to see his sin for what it is and then turns against it in his heart with real hatred and sorrow and shame, confesses it with his lips, and turns away from it in deed.

Chapter 2

A Heart of Flesh

Then I will give them one heart, and I will put a new spirit
within them, and take the stony heart out of their flesh,
and give them a heart of flesh. (Ezekiel 11:19)

In Ezekiel 11:19, God promises to remove the heart of stone from His people and give them a heart of flesh. This passage speaks of a profound inner transformation by which a person's hard, impermeable heart gives way and suddenly becomes sensitive to the things of God. This chapter will discuss this metamorphosis—its effects, origin, necessity, and continuation.

Specific Effects of Repentance

Let's first explore some of the specific effects that genuine repentance produces in a person's heart and life. While we might rightly attribute these effects to regeneration in general, I think it will be of some benefit to connect them particularly to the grace of repentance so we can identify them (or lack thereof) in ourselves and others.

One of the most profound effects of repentance in the heart is the cultivation of contentment. Repentance teaches a person that he deserves nothing from God but eternal punishment because of his grievous sin and inward corruption. It's not that he *expects* hell—for he knows that repentance is unto eternal life (Acts 11:18)—but he knows that he *deserves* it. Therefore, he can be content with whatever God gives him. He knows it is better than what his wickedness has merited.

To illustrate this concept, imagine a criminal who is on death row for some horrific, high-profile crime he committed. But while he is awaiting execution, he renounces his former way of life, turning over a new leaf, so to speak. Word of his transformation spreads, and moments before his execution he receives word that he has been pardoned by the president. He knows he deserves the death penalty for his crime, but he now expects he will not receive it—to his inexpressible gratitude.

This man now experiences (to the extent that he remembers his former plight) unshakable contentment, even amid terrible circumstances. If prison guards take away his mattress and he must sleep on the floor of his cell, he will be content, because he recognizes he doesn't deserve even a floor to sleep on. If they feed him nothing but bread, he will remain content, for he knows he doesn't deserve even bread to eat. So it is with the true penitent.

Another way in which repentance produces contentment in the heart is by concurrently working humility. The person who rightly knows his own heart necessarily holds himself in low esteem; he views himself as low, weak, dependent, and unimportant. He is the worst sinner that he knows, for he is acutely aware of the plank in his own eye, while only seeing a speck in his brother's eye (Matt. 7:3). And, as Jeremiah Burroughs put it, "A man who is little in his own eyes will count every affliction as little, and every mercy as great."[1] Burroughs notes that Saul, when he was small in his own eyes, was unaffected by the fact that some people rejected him as king. But when his heart had

---

[1] Jeremiah Burroughs, *The Rare Jewel of Christian Contentment* (Edinburgh: Banner of Truth, 1964), 89.

become inflated with pride, it infuriated him to hear the people singing, "Saul has slain his thousands, and David his ten thousands" (1 Sam. 18:7).

Contrast Saul's pride-generated discontentment with David's humility-wrought contentment, which he displayed when faced with a far greater personal affront. In 2 Samuel 16:5–13, we learn that upon Absalom's usurpation of the throne, David was forced to flee Jerusalem. When he entered the town of Bahurim, a man named Shimei began hurling curses at him, calling him a "rogue" and a "bloodthirsty man." Abishai, one of David's loyal soldiers, offered to kill him on the spot. David, without a doubt, would have been justified to give his assent. However, he did not. Instead, he responded, "What have I to do with you, you sons of Zeruiah? So let him curse, because the LORD has said to him, 'Curse David.' Who then shall say, 'Why have you done so?'" (v. 10). David had indeed shed innocent blood when he gave the order for Uriah to be killed, and through the repentance that followed, God had thoroughly humbled him. It was on this basis that he was able to contentedly bear Shimei's curses.

Repentance inevitably has this contentment-producing effect on all who experience it (though it is nonetheless their duty to do all they can to cultivate it). Their humble view of themselves enables them to remain content while they are defamed, dishonored, and disrespected. When they feel the first rumblings of discontent because of slander or mistreatment, they remind themselves, "If they could fully see the corruption of my heart, they would justifiably hurl stones at me along with their insults."

The humbling effect of repentance will also be seen in the penitent's thoughts toward, and treatment of, others. When he sees someone trapped in sin, he will pity and pray for him rather than become frustrated or scornful, for he remembers he was once entangled in sin and, apart from God's intervention, he would have remained in it.

Furthermore, his grief over sin is not confined to that which he sees in himself but extends to the sins he sees committed around him. The prophet Daniel fasted and wept over the sins of his people, confessing them before God (Dan. 9). The prophet Ezekiel saw a vision in which God commanded five angels to go throughout Jerusalem and slaughter every man, woman, and child. But before they went to carry out his orders, God told another angel:

> Go through the midst of the city, through the midst of Jerusalem, and put a mark on the foreheads of the men who sigh and cry over all the abominations that are done within it. . . . Utterly slay old and young men, maidens and little children and women; but do not come near anyone on whom is the mark; and begin at My sanctuary." So they began with the elders who were before the temple. (Ezek. 9:4, 6)

Notice the distinguishing characteristic of those who are to be spared from his wrath: they "sigh and cry" over the wickedness they see around them. They mourn over sin, not because of a sense of obligation or external compulsion but because they see it for what it is. And by their outward grief, they demonstrate their hearts are aligned with the heart of God.

Imagine, if you will, the responses they must have evoked in the people around them. Some probably mocked and scoffed at the sight of them. Others were likely indignant, even angry, labeling them self-righteous and legalistic. But perhaps the more pious of their peers said things like, "Where is your joy?" and "Don't worry, God will show us mercy; we *are* His chosen people." Maybe some even patronized them, asking the mourners to pray for them, then plunging themselves right back into their sin. But the people's apathy, pride, and presumption did nothing to quiet the troubled hearts of the righteous. They continued to groan under the burden of the sins of their nation—to their own deliverance.

The Source of Repentance

Whenever a change takes place, there must be something behind it. Newton's first law of motion, which says that a body in motion tends to stay in motion unless acted upon by an external force, might appropriately be applied to the realm of the human heart. Scripture says that the mass of fallen humanity is going in the wrong direction. We are "by nature objects of wrath" who, though we know God, do not glorify Him as God (Rom. 1:18, 21). We love our sin and have no desire for the divine light to expose it for what it is. So we reject God and walk—no, run—on the broad path that leads away from Him. What, then, is the external force that acts on a soul in such motion and changes its course? Scripture is clear that the ultimate source is not a crisis event or even good preaching but God Himself. Consider the following passages:

- "Him God has exalted to His right hand to be Prince and Savior, to give repentance to Israel and forgiveness of sins" (Acts 5:31).

- "When they heard these things they became silent; and they glorified God, saying, 'Then God has also granted to the Gentiles repentance to life'" (Acts 11:18).

- "In humility correcting those who are in opposition, if God perhaps will grant them repentance, so that they may know the truth" (2 Tim. 2:25).

All three passages speak of God giving or granting people repentance. The implication here is that He is the sole source of this grace and no one can repent unless God enables him to do so.

One of the ways in which God enables repentance is by teaching a person to fear Him, which cultivates the soil of the heart, preparing it for the seed of repentance. But it is important to note there are

33

different ways in which one might fear God, and not all of them are conducive to repentance. Take, for example, the self-centered, cringing kind of fear that King Saul exhibited when the prophet Samuel confronted him with his sin of not destroying the Amalekites. Saul clung to Samuel's robe, begging him to grant forgiveness on God's behalf because he feared that God would take the kingdom from him because of his sin.

But the fear of God that leads to repentance is centered on Him and rooted in the apprehension of His holy hatred toward sin and His righteous wrath that will be poured out on sinners. This type of fear is, in the words of John Bunyan, "an effect of sound awakenings by the word of wrath which begetteth in the soul a sense of its right to eternal damnation."[2] In other words, it does not result from one simply believing he is going to suffer in hell but from understanding that God will be completely just in sending him there to experience His wrath for all eternity because he has broken God's law. The "word of wrath" of which Bunyan speaks is the promise of divine judgment toward all who live in rebellion against God. Some of the many iterations of this promise can be found in passages like Exodus 22:24, 2 Chronicles 30:8, Proverbs 11:23, Isaiah 13:9, John 3:36, Colossians 3:6, and Romans 1:18, to name a few.

When some people read these verses or hear them preached, their souls are stirred, and they are filled with the fear of the Lord. But others continue in their state of spiritual slumber after reading and hearing them countless times. For it is not the verses alone that teach this fear but the Holy Spirit working through and alongside the Word that awakens the heart. John 16:8–11 tells us that it is the Holy Spirit who convicts sinners of their wickedness and convinces them of the judgment of God that will come upon them. He thus instills godly fear

---

[2] John Bunyan, *The Works of John Bunyan,* ed. George Offor (Glasgow: Blackie and Son, 1858), 448.

in those whom He desires to bring to repentance. Calvin put it this way: "We cannot be trained to the fear of God . . . unless we are violently smitten with the sword of the Spirit and annihilated."[3] God is the initiator and instructor of the kind of fear of Him that leads to repentance. He is therefore the source of repentance itself.

Another indication God is the author of repentance is that we are told in Scripture He gives people His Spirit, which produces in them a new heart, a "heart of flesh" to replace their "heart of stone" (Ezek. 36:26). The stony heart is unwilling, indeed unable, to respond to God because it is hard and lifeless. It is the kind of heart the Jews demonstrated when God called them to return to Him, and they said, "In what way shall we return?" (Mal. 3:7). Their problem was not simply that they were wicked and idolatrous but that they were incapable of seeing they had turned away from God. There was no spiritual sensitivity, no sign of life in their hearts. Paul refers to this kind of person as the "natural man" and says he "does not receive the things of the Spirit of God, for they are foolishness to him; nor can he know them, because they are spiritually discerned" (1 Cor. 2:14). So the natural, or stony-hearted, man may hear that he is a sinner destined for hell because he has violated God's commands, and he may hear the command to repent of his sins—yet he is unable to repent because he is blind to the fact that his way of life is abominable to God.

The only way this man can repent is if God imparts to him a heart of flesh that can sense his own spiritual condition and is able to grieve over and hate his sin. The words of the classic hymn "Jesus Paid It All" portray this concept beautifully:

> Lord, now indeed I find
> Thy pow'r, and Thine alone,

---

[3] John Calvin, *Institutes of the Christian Religion*, trans. Henry Beveridge (Grand Rapids, MI: Eerdmans, 1997), 515.

> Can change the leopard's spots
> And melt the heart of stone.

But some might wonder how it could be that God is the sole author of repentance, granting it to some and not to others, when the apostle Peter tells us that God is "not willing that any should perish, but that all should come to repentance" (2 Peter 3:9). This is a valid question, and it must be answered in several parts. First, no orthodox Christian maintains that everyone experiences repentance. So the fact that some people do not repent means that God's desire for all men to repent is not being carried out. However, we are also told in Scripture God ensures all His purposes are accomplished (Isa. 43:13; 46:9–10). How then can God's will be done in one sense and not in another? Theologian I. Howard Marshall writes: "To avoid all misconceptions, it should be made clear at the outset that the fact that God wishes or wills that all people should be saved does not necessarily imply that all will respond to the gospel and be saved. We must certainly distinguish between what God would like to see happen and what he actually does will to happen, and both of these things can be spoken of as God's will."[4]

On the one hand, the thing that God would like to see happen has been called God's *will of command*, or His *revealed will*. One example of this is when He told Pharaoh, through Moses, to let the Hebrews go. On the other hand, the thing that God actually wills and causes to happen has been referred to as His *will of decree*, or His *secret will*. This is seen when He tells Moses, "And I will harden Pharaoh's heart, and multiply My signs and My wonders in the land of Egypt" (Ex. 7:3). So, it is biblically accurate to say that God wants everyone to repent and come to eternal life, while at the same time He does not grant repentance to everyone.

---

[4] Quoted in John Piper, *Does God Desire All to Be Saved?* (Wheaton: Crossway Books, 2013), 18.

How then could Christ command people to do something they cannot do in their own strength or by their own will? After all, it wouldn't be fair to command a quadriplegic to get up and walk or a dead person to come back to life—their obedience is impossible. But commanding such things is exactly what we see Jesus doing throughout the Gospels. "Lazarus, come out!" and to the paralytic, "Take up your mat and walk," are unfair imperatives if the subject is expected to obey without divine assistance. If the paralytic's legs were not strengthened by Christ's power simultaneously with His command, he could not have obeyed. Similarly, if Lazarus was not brought to life to hear Jesus's words, he would have been unable to respond. In Romans 4 we are told that God brings the dead to life and calls the things that are not as though they were. That is His prerogative.

So it is with the call to repentance (and faith). When someone responds to Christ's call, it is the spiritual equivalent of three-days-dead Lazarus walking out of his tomb. When they hear it, they realize they are alive and able—indeed, inclined—to respond. Jesus says that His sheep, and only His sheep, hear His voice. The Pharisees did not believe because they were not Christ's sheep. It's not that they heard His voice and wanted to follow but were unable. Rather, they did not hear His voice at all because they only knew the voice of their own shepherd: Satan.

Yet their inability to hear Christ's voice does not take away their responsibility—the Bible is unequivocal regarding the eternal destiny of all who reject the gospel. Here we have, as J. I. Packer observes in *Evangelism and the Sovereignty of God*, an antinomy, "an appearance of contradiction between conclusions which seem equally logical, reasonable or necessary." It "is neither dispensable nor comprehensible. . . . We do not invent it, and we cannot explain it." God "orders and controls all things, human actions among them" but "He holds every man responsible for the choices he makes and the courses of action he pursues." Packer concludes, "To our finite minds, of course, the thing is inexplicable."[5]

The Necessity of Repentance

The next facet of repentance is its necessity in salvation. That it is indeed necessary to repent is evident from many passages of Scripture. Jesus commanded His hearers to repent (Mark 1:15); in fact, calling sinners to repentance was an integral part of His earthly ministry (Luke 5:32). Jesus warned people of the consequences of their continued impenitence: "Unless you repent you will all likewise perish" (Luke 13:3). Moreover, Jesus exhorted His disciples to preach "repentance and remission of sins . . . in His name to all nations" (Luke 24:47). The connection between repentance and forgiveness of sins is explicit in this passage, as well as in Acts 5:31. It is therefore also linked to eternal life (Acts 11:18), as only those whose sins have been forgiven can experience the life of God. Furthermore, the author of Hebrews identifies repentance as part of the foundation of the faith (Heb. 6:1). Clearly, without repentance, one cannot be saved.

Let's now examine the reasons why repentance is an indispensable part of salvation.[6] First, repentance prepares the way for Christ in the heart. John the Baptist is identified in all four Gospels as the fulfillment of Isaiah's prophecy: "The voice of one crying in the wilderness: 'Prepare the way of the LORD; Make His paths straight'" (Mark 1:3; see also Matt. 3:3; Luke 3:4; John 1:23). The metaphor of *preparing the way* comes from the fact that in the ancient world most roads were constructed of dirt or gravel and were poorly maintained.

---

[5] J. I. Packer, *Evangelism and the Sovereignty of God* (Downers Grove, IL: Intervarsity, 2008), 23, 26–28.

[6] R. C. Sproul refers to repentance as a prerequisite, a necessary condition for salvation (*Essential Truths of the Christian Faith*, Carol Stream, IL: Tyndale House, 1992, 203). I disagree with this position as it is more accurate, I think, to consider it a part of salvation. In granting a person repentance, God has already begun the work of saving him. See also Spurgeon's sermon "Repentance to Life."

If a king or important dignitary was going to travel any great distance, servants would go ahead of him to ensure there were no holes or obstructions in the road that would impede or endanger him. Heralds would also precede the king to inform the inhabitants of the destination city that he was coming.[7]

John's mission was to prepare the way for Christ, the Lord, the King of Glory, not by preparing literal roads but by making ready the hearts of the people to receive Him. He accomplished this by "preaching a baptism of repentance" (Luke 3:3), for it is in repenting that a person sees his true spiritual condition—that he is corrupt through and through, that he is without hope, that he is sick in the most profound sense. This is essential to receiving Jesus, because, as the Lord says, "Those who are well have no need of a physician, but those who are sick" (Luke 5:31). In short, repentance is intimately connected with faith in Christ.

The repentance-faith connection is an important concept and is worth exploring in some depth. Repentance and faith are the two sides of the coin of salvation—they are two graces that go hand in hand, and a person cannot experience one without the other. Jesus's command to "Repent, and believe in the gospel" (Mark 1:15) explicitly testifies to this, as do passages like Acts 20:21 and Hebrews 6:1. The reasons for this relationship are several.

First, both are the gift of God through the working of the Holy Spirit in a person's heart. Regarding *faith*, Paul writes in his letter to the church in Ephesus, "For by grace you have been saved through faith, and that not of yourselves; it is the gift of God" (Eph. 2:8). We are told throughout the New Testament that whoever believes on the Lord

---

[7] John H. Walton, Victor H. Matthews, and Mark W. Chavalas, *The IVP Bible Background Commentary: Old Testament* (Downers Grove, IL: Intervarsity, 2000), 625.

Jesus Christ will be saved. This fact is used by many to justify the current evangelical trends some refer to as "easy-believism" and "decisionism." I will explore these concepts later, but it will suffice for now to say both stem from the assumption that believing on Christ is essentially an assent to several core doctrines—namely, Jesus Christ was God in the flesh, lived a sinless life, died on the cross for the forgiveness of sins, and was resurrected on the third day.

To be sure, holding to the orthodox tenets of the faith is part of true belief, but it is not the sum of it. James tells us demons believe these things and shudder (James 2:19). In fact, Satan's theological views are more accurate than the most learned Christian scholar; he saw God's face as he ministered before Him day and night. Not only do demons believe right things about God, they also obey Him, worship Him, and make requests of Him (Mark 5:7). These are all things a person can choose to do. They require no divine assistance, no overt working of the Holy Spirit.

What then is the saving faith that is produced in the heart by the Holy Spirit? Jonathan Edwards asserts it is "the sense of the heart, wherein the mind does not only speculate and behold but relishes and feels."[8] It is to have a new sense, new taste buds in the heart, which are sensible to the sweetness of God, as the tongue detects the sweetness of honey and the eyes perceive the beauty of a rainbow. One might have a great notional understanding of honey's sweetness without ever having tasted it. But the person who has eaten honey, though he knows little else about it, has greater understanding and more accurate beliefs about it. In short, faith involves not only assent to facts but also affections and inclinations of the heart. And while faith includes love for and attraction to Christ, the object of faith, true repentance entails hatred and revulsion of sin. For the one who has received the grace of faith sees God as He is—holy, pure, gracious,

[8] Jonathan Edwards, *Religious Affections* (Carlisle, PA: Banner of Truth, 1997), 198.

and loving—and his heart is drawn to Him. But his eyes are also opened to see his own sin and corruption.

Or, to put it another way, repentance and faith are the result of instant inward conformity to God, which the Spirit produces in a person's heart when he is born again, causing him to be sensitive to and to hate that which God hates (repentance) and to perceive and love the perfections of God (faith). While this conformity to God's heart is not perfected in this life, it begins at regeneration and continues through the sanctification process.

In the Old Testament, saving faith was demonstrated in an apprehension of the glory of God in His law and covenant: "Your testimonies are wonderful; therefore my soul keeps them" (Ps. 119:129). Notice that the emphasis is not on the action but on the state of heart by which the action is produced. For New Testament believers, the excellence of God is most thoroughly manifested in Jesus Christ, and faith is the beholding of "the light of the knowledge of the glory of God" in His face (2 Cor. 4:6). This inward conformity to the heart of God begins in man's innermost being at regeneration and advances into the periphery through the process of sanctification. It is not completed in this life but will be when we see Him face to face (1 John 3:2).

Another connection between repentance and faith is that repentance enables faith (according to the definition of faith I've suggested, in which one doesn't merely assent to the reality of Christ but is drawn to Him and sees Him as precious) in the sense that repentance makes the gospel exceedingly sweet and attractive. When a person sees his sin in the light of God's holiness, he is, like Peter's listeners in Acts 4, "cut to the heart" and wonders if there is any remedy for his miserable condition. When he discovers there is indeed a remedy and that it is found in the death and resurrection of Jesus Christ, he becomes captivated by Christ and experiences genuine faith.

Notice this pattern also in the account of Augustine of Hippo of his own conversion:

> How sweet did it suddenly become to me to be without the sweetness of trifles! And it was now a joy to put away what I formerly feared to lose. For you cast them away from me, true and highest sweetness. You cast them away, and in their place you entered in yourself—sweeter than all pleasure. . . . Now was my soul free from the gnawing cares of seeking and getting, of wallowing in the mire and scratching the itch of lust. And I prattled like a child to you, Lord my God—my light, my riches, and my salvation.[9]

By his own account, Augustine had led a lecherous life before his conversion. He moved out of his parents' house at the age of sixteen to live with his girlfriend, and for the next fifteen years was a slave to lust. Then one day he was sitting with friends when someone showed up at the house and shared with him the testimony of a well-known Christian. God used this testimony to bring Augustine to repentance and faith. For him, repentance meant his eyes being opened in an instant to see his lust as "trifles" and "mire." That which he once clung to with all his might became to him leprous and filthy. And at the same time, faith entered his heart, making Christ "sweeter than all pleasure" to the taste buds of his heart. Certainly, not every conversion is as dramatic as Augustine's, but every true conversion does bear witness to the relationship between faith and repentance.

The Continuation of Repentance

Up to this point, I have been referring to the initial repentance that accompanies faith as part of conversion—the point at which a person is justified, when his sin is transferred to Christ on the cross and Christ's righteousness is imputed to him. But now I would like to

---

[9] Saint Augustine, *Confessions*, trans. Albert C. Outler (New York: Barnes and Noble, 1997), 128.

discuss repentance as it relates to sanctification—the lifelong process by which one is conformed to the image of Christ. In this regard, repentance is ongoing. Jesus's command to repent is in the present imperative tense in the Greek, which means He is commanding His hearers to repent *continually*. Martin Luther said, in the first of his ninety-five theses, that the entire life of believers should be repentance.

So, we are not finished repenting after our conversion but are drawn by the Holy Spirit into ever-increasing depths of repentance. The same Spirit who opened our eyes to see our sin and corruption, stirred our soul against it, and enabled us to turn away from it will continue this work until the day we are finally perfected in the presence of God (Phil. 1:6). Perfect repentance is not possible in this life—as long as we are chained to this body of flesh, we will not be able to fully turn from our sin. Nevertheless, we should continually strive against sin while petitioning God for the grace necessary to overcome it.

One might wonder why God doesn't grant the believer full repentance at the onset of his journey. I think that at least part of the reason can be found in Exodus 23:29–30. In this passage, God told the Israelites He was going to bring them into Canaan and drive out the other nations from before them—but He was not going to do this all at once: "I will not drive them out from before you in one year, lest the land become desolate and the beasts of the field become too numerous for you. Little by little I will drive them out from before you, until you have increased, and you inherit the land." In other words, the land was too large for the Israelites to occupy at their present size. So He promised to drive out the people one at a time so that by the time they were all gone the population of Israel would be sufficient to fill the land.

Similarly, when God brings us, as believers, out of bondage to sin and into spiritual Canaan, He does not drive out all the corruption at once. For the land is large, so to speak, and the indwelling word is but a seedling. Christ is yet to be fully formed in us (Gal. 4:19). But it is nevertheless certain that God will ultimately drive out all our enemies and enable us to possess the vast and fruitful land He has promised.

Perpetual penitence does not mean the Christian constantly hangs his head in sadness and self-loathing. There are times when (figurative) sackcloth and ashes are appropriate, but in general, the soul that is weighed down by ever-increasing awareness of his sin and sadness over it will be buoyed up by a perpetually greater and more compelling view of Christ and deeper trust in Him. The apostle Paul describes and models for us this balance in Romans 7:

> For what I am doing, I do not understand. For what I will to do, that I do not practice; but what I hate, that I do. . . . For I know that in me (that is, in my flesh) nothing good dwells; for to will is present with me, but how to perform what is good I do not find. For the good that I will to do, I do not do; but the evil I will not to do, that I practice. . . . But I see another law in my members, warring against the law of my mind, and bringing me into captivity to the law of sin which is in my members. O wretched man that I am! Who will deliver me from this body of death? I thank God—through Jesus Christ our Lord! So then, with the mind I myself serve the law of God, but with the flesh the law of sin. (vv. 15, 18–19, 23–25) [10]

Paul, one of the most eminent saints in the history of the church, continued to see his sin more vividly and in greater depth. Moreover, he hated it and was grieved over it, considering it a loathsome and heavy affliction. The Greek word *talaiporos*, which is translated "wretched" in verse 24, indicates an enormously, almost crushingly,

---

[10] Some have suggested that Paul is here describing an unbeliever, but I do not find their arguments compelling. The apostle says in verse 22 he delights in the law of the Lord in the inner man, which an unbeliever certainly cannot do, according to the first three chapters of the same epistle.

heavy trial. Up to this point, the reader might wonder how Paul could even be describing the experience of a Christian, much less a man like himself. But in the same instant that his soul was brought low by an accurate view of self, he was elevated to dazzling heights as he considered the sufficiency and power of Christ to rescue him from his "body of death."

This was also one of the defining marks of the Puritans. They possessed an outward austerity that is disconcerting to many in the modern church. But what many do not realize is that the austerity and solemnity of these spiritual giants was largely superficial, and they had a deep, robust joy rooted in their total dependence on Christ. We would do well to learn from them.

So we see that as we Christians are sanctified by the power of God, the taste buds of our hearts become more sensitive to the bitterness of sin, and our repentance is therefore deepened. But the capacity of these taste buds to perceive the sweetness of Jesus Christ is simultaneously increased, bringing the perpetually penitent to ever-greater heights of joy and satisfaction in Christ. Doddridge poetically conveys this paradoxical reality in his classic hymn, "Repent the Voice Celestial Cries":

> Repent, the voice celestial cries,
> Nor longer dare delay:
> The wretch that scorns the mandate dies,
> And meets a fiery day.
>
> No more the sovereign eye of God
> O'er looks the crimes of men;
> His heralds are dispatched abroad
> To warn the world of sin.
>
> Together in his presence bow,
> And all your guilt confess;
> Accept the offered savior now,
> Nor trifle with his grace.

Bow, ere the awful trumpet sound,
And call you to his bar;
For mercy knows the appointed bound,
And turns to vengeance there.

Amazing love, that yet will call,
And yet prolong our days!
Our hearts subdued by goodness fall,
And weep, and love, and praise.

Chapter 3

Possible Objections

But declared first to those in Damascus and in Jerusalem, and throughout all the region of Judea, and then to the Gentiles, that they should repent, turn to God, and do works befitting repentance. (Acts 26:20)

The wise King Solomon once observed, "The first one to plead his cause seems right, until his neighbor comes and examines him" (Prov. 18:17). The view of repentance conveyed here may seem biblically sound, but it may be wondered whether it can withstand scrutiny. In this chapter, I will discuss and attempt to answer common objections.

It's Too Complex

One objection sometimes expressed to this view of repentance is that it is unnecessarily complex: "Doesn't the Bible state that 'if you confess with your mouth the Lord Jesus and believe in your heart that God has raised Him from the dead, you will be saved' (Rom. 10:9)?"

Writing a book about repentance is somewhat akin to writing a book on swimming the backstroke using only words and no pictures. Regardless of the skill of the author, the non-swimming reader would almost certainly consider the backstroke to be a very difficult and complex activity. And in one sense, it is; there are fine points that require lots of instruction and practice to master. But to learn the basic form and motion, one hour spent in the pool with the swimming instructor will probably suffice.

This fact notwithstanding, the book is not without value. First, it imparts to the reader enough knowledge of the backstroke that he will probably not confuse it with the dog paddle, which he already knows how to do. And reading the book has probably given him enough of a right conception of the breaststroke that when he learns to do it, he'll know that he is doing it correctly. He will most likely say to himself at some point, "Oh, that's what the book was saying!" Additionally, experienced swimmers will probably find the book helpful in that they might learn something that makes their own movement more efficient or enables them to teach others using clearer and more accurate terminology.

Likewise, I do not expect this book on repentance to teach people how to repent; God is the only instructor qualified to do that. And when He does, it will not seem at all complex or confusing, as it may appear in the abstract. Nevertheless, it is, in my estimation, worth delineating the different aspects of repentance as they are presented in Scripture. It would serve no one to dilute the truth for the sake of simplicity. Confessing Christ with the lips and believing in Him in the heart is indeed the way in which one is saved, but we must understand this truth in such a way that it includes all the other things the Bible speaks of concerning the salvation of souls, such as repentance (Luke 13:5), obedience (Heb. 5:9), humility (Matt. 18:4), and love (1 Cor. 13:1–3).

A person must come to Christ on Christ's terms if he is to come to Him at all. Few people seek Christ in the right way because few desire Him for the right reasons. In Luke 4:18, Jesus describes four kinds of people who are truly prepared to receive Him: "The Spirit of the LORD is upon Me, because He has anointed Me to preach the gospel to the poor; He has sent Me to heal the brokenhearted, to proclaim liberty to the captives and recovery of sight to the blind, to set at liberty those who are oppressed."

Here, Jesus was reading from Isaiah 61 in the synagogue, and then He tells His audience that the prophet's words have been fulfilled in their hearing. In other words, He is the one who has been anointed by the Spirit to preach the gospel to the poor, heal the brokenhearted, preach deliverance to captives, and give sight to the blind. These are the four basic groups to whom Jesus has something to offer.

It is vitally important to our understanding of true repentance that we interpret these categories not in the literal, physical sense (e.g., material poverty) but in the spiritual sense. Those who fail to do so invariably twist the true gospel into the "social gospel," making man's physical needs the central issue and his spiritual needs the peripheral. While it is true that Jesus had compassion on the physically poor and infirmed (He cared for people's bodies), His primary objective was to bring souls into the kingdom of God. It is also worth noting here that the conditions of physical poverty, sickness, and dejectedness—things that Christians of the past called "crosses"—while not being of any spiritual value in and of themselves, can be a cause of restlessness and discomfort which God may use as a spur to cause a person to pursue spiritual things.

The Poor in Spirit

The kind of poverty to which Jesus refers is spiritual poverty, and it is the mark of those "blessed" ones to whom belongs the kingdom of heaven (Matt. 5:3). It does not naturally exist in the human heart, regardless of socioeconomic status, but must be wrought by the Holy Spirit. Those who possess this posture of heart recognize that they have nothing to commend themselves to Christ—not one ounce of righteousness and not a single good deed. They approach Christ empty-handedly to "buy wine and milk without money and without price" (Isa. 55:1). The late A. W. Pink affirms this view of spiritual poverty in his work on the Sermon on the Mount:

Poverty of spirit is a consciousness of my emptiness, the result of the Spirit's work within. It issues from the painful discovery that all my righteousnesses are as filthy rags. It follows the awakening that my best performances are unacceptable, yea, an abomination to the thrice Holy One. Poverty of spirit evidences itself by its bringing the individual into the dust before God, acknowledging his utter helplessness and deservingness of hell. ... [The spiritually poor] take the place of beggars, are glad to receive Divine charity, and begin to seek true riches. ... [They] have the Gospel ... preached not only to their ears, but to their hearts![1]

Puritan Richard Sibbes astutely links the spiritually poor man to the "bruised reed" and the "smoking flax" which Jesus says He will not break or quench (Matt. 12:20):

He is sensible of sin and misery, even unto bruising; and, seeing no help in himself, is carried with restless desire to have supply from another, with some hope, which a little raises him out of himself to Christ. ... This spark of hope being opposed by doubtings and fears rising from corruption makes him as smoking flax; so that both these together make up the state of a poor distressed man. This is such an one as our Saviour Christ terms "poor in spirit."[2]

The Brokenhearted

The second category of people who may rightly receive Christ are the brokenhearted. This state of heart and mind is totally unrelated to modern connotations of the term *broken heart*, which are mostly linked with broken relationships, unmet desires, unfulfilled aspirations, and the like. Just as the word *poor* must be understood in the spiritual sense, so must *brokenhearted*. Those of whom Jesus speaks are broken over their sin. They are sad with the "godly sorrow"

---

[1] A. W. Pink, *An Exposition of the Sermon on the Mount* (Grand Rapids: Baker, 1995), 296.

[2] Richard Sibbes, *The Bruised Reed* (Edinburgh: Banner of Truth, 2011), 4.

that Paul speaks of in 2 Corinthians 7:10 (see chapter 1 for elaboration on this).

Those whose hearts are broken over their sin and corruption are in exactly the right place for receiving healing from Christ. When the Samaritan woman asked Jesus for some of the living water of which He spoke, He told her to go get her husband (John 4:16), which must have been for her like touching an open nerve. The Great Physician showed the patient the seriousness of her wound, and then she was able to properly come to Him for healing. For, as Jesus tells the Pharisees, "Those who are well have no need of a physician, but those who are sick" (Luke 5:31).

The Captives

The third group to whom Jesus was anointed to preach are the captives, and His message to them is one of liberty. Once again, this should be construed primarily in the spiritual sense. Those who are prepared to hear and receive Jesus's proclamation of liberty are those who groan under their bondage to sin (Rom. 6:16; John 8:34) and long to be freed from its guilt and power. Matthew Henry writes concerning this verse:

> The gospel is a proclamation of liberty, like that to Israel in Egypt and in Babylon. By the merit of Christ sinners may be loosed from the bonds of guilt, and by his Spirit and grace from the bondage of corruption. It is a deliverance from the worst of thraldoms, which all those shall have the benefit of that are willing to make Christ their Head, and are willing to be ruled by him.[3]

Those who are either unaware of their bondage to sin or indifferent about it are in no position to hear the gospel of freedom. Had the

---

[3] Matthew Henry, *Matthew Henry's Commentary on the Whole Bible* (Peabody, MA: Hendrickson, 1996), 1837.

Israelites in Egypt not yearned for freedom, God's promise to bring them out through Moses would have fallen on deaf ears.

The Blind

Finally, Jesus was sent to "proclaim . . . recovery of sight to the blind." Notice that it does not say that Jesus was sent to *restore* sight to the blind, which He of course did, in the physical sense. Rather, Jesus was sent to—and did—proclaim to the spiritually blind the good news of restored vision.

Spiritual sight is the ability to perceive with the eyes of the heart such spiritual realities as the glory of God and the heinousness of sin. Nobody is born with this kind of sight. Like newborn rabbits we are born with our spiritual eyelids fused shut and must have them opened by God. But not everyone is aware that they cannot see. In fact, many become filled with indignation at the suggestion that they are blind. John informs us this was precisely the case with the Pharisees:

> Jesus said, "For judgment I have come into this world, that those who do not see may see, and that those who see may be made blind." Then some of the Pharisees who were with Him heard these words, and said to Him, "Are we blind also?" Jesus said to them, "If you were blind, you would have no sin; but now you say, 'We see.' Therefore your sin remains." (John 9:39–41)

The Pharisees considered their vision to be perfect and were incredulous when Jesus implied they were blind. So it is with all who fail to recognize their own spiritual blindness. They continue to walk in utter oblivion down the path of destruction until they are plummeted into hell. But to those who acknowledge and mourn over their blindness, Christ's message is truly good news. Therefore, they, along with the poor, the brokenhearted, and the captives, are able to rightly receive Christ.

It's Not Always Like That

Another challenge to this view of repentance is that not everyone in the New Testament experiences repentance as I have defined it—that is, sight, sorrow, hatred, shame, confession, turning. I agree there are several cases in Scripture that are portrayed as genuine conversions, in which one or more characteristics of repentance are not seen. The accounts of the Samaritan woman at the well (John 4:11), the Ethiopian eunuch (Acts 8:30), and the thief on the cross (Luke 23:43) are a few notable examples that seem to undermine my definition of repentance.

However, if it is true that repentance occurs primarily in the heart, as I have suggested, then we should not expect it to be outwardly visible. To be sure, we will often see external indications of what is transpiring in someone's heart, but even those will vary from person to person. How could the Samaritan woman not have been ashamed for her sin when confronted with it by the Messiah? How could the Ethiopian eunuch not have grieved over the sin for which the Servant of Isaiah 53 was crushed by God? And would not the thief on the cross have turned from his sin and lived for God if he were given the chance?

Furthermore, not everyone is brought under the same degree of conviction for their sin; the Holy Spirit does not work in the heart of every person in the same way. This is affirmed by Spurgeon in a message titled "Repentance unto Life":

> Repentance is a hatred of sin, and a forsaking it. It is possible for a man to repent without any terrific display of the terrors of the law; he may repent without having heard the trumpet sounds of Sinai, without having heard more than a distant rumble of its thunder. A man may repent entirely through the power of the voice of mercy. Some hearts God opens to faith, as in the case of Lydia. Others he assaults with the sledge hammer of the wrath to come; some he opens with the picklock of grace, and some with the crowbar of the law. There may be different ways of getting

there, but the question is, has he got there? Is he there? It often happens that the Lord is not in the tempest or in the earthquake, but in the "still small voice."[4]

David Brainerd, the famous eighteenth-century missionary to the American Indians, also attests to this:

> And that which has distressed many of them under convictions is, that they found they wanted, and could not obtain, the happiness of the godly; at least they have often appeared to be more affected with this, than with the terrors of hell. But whatever be the means of their awakening, it is plain, numbers are made deeply sensible of their sin and misery, the wickedness and stubbornness of their own hearts, their utter inability to help themselves, or to come to Christ for help, without divine assistance; and so are brought to see their perishing need of Christ to do all for them, and to lie at the foot of sovereign mercy.[5]

In short, some are brought to repentance when they see their abject wickedness for what it is and that they are suspended over the flames of hell by a thread. Others repent when they glimpse the beauty and excellence of Christ and mourn the fact that their sin and unbelief keep them from Him. Circumstances, means, and outward displays of repentance are unimportant. What matters is that true repentance is experienced.

Broken Heart or Wounded Pride

Another argument that might be raised is people today already feel badly enough about themselves. They need a spiritual boost, not a beating. They need someone to love on them, not tell them to feel bad about their sin.

---

[4] "Repentance unto Life," Sermon No. 44, The Spurgeon Center, accessed December 21, 2017, https://www.spurgeon.org/resource-library/sermons.

[5] Jonathan Edwards, *The Life and Diary of David Brainerd* (Chicago: Moody, 1980), 256–57.

To this I respond that Jesus, the most loving person who ever lived, commanded people to repent or be eternally damned. Therefore, any form of love that excludes exhorting perishing people to spiritual brokenness is deficient at best and homicidal at worst. For when we proclaim to sinners the good news of salvation through faith in Jesus Christ but do not exhort them to repentance, we give them only a half-gospel and, therefore, do them great harm.

Further, people's bad feelings about themselves are often rooted in pride. I'll borrow an analogy from John Piper to illustrate this fact:

> Suppose you go to a dinner party and find out when you get there that you are dressed wrong; and then you spill your coffee; and then you don't know which fork to pick up first; and then the joke you attempt falls flat; and when you are leaving, you call your hostess by the wrong name. How do you feel about yourself when you get home? Rotten. You hate yourself. You're depressed. You don't want to show your face. You feel like quitting your job. What's the use when you're such a klutz? Now I ask, where does all that low self-image come from? Whence all these depressing, immobilizing, self-denouncing feelings? Is the answer: God's offended glory or your offended pride? People who are depressed and immobilized and angry because their behavior has injured the glory of God are very, very rare. But people who are depressed and immobilized and angry because their behavior has prevented them from having a reputation of being cool and competent are very, very common.[6]

The penitent sinner will indeed feel bad about himself, but the Holy Spirit is at work in his heart and will raise up his soul, for repentance is part of the crucifixion of the "old man" that Paul speaks of in Romans 6. And no one would seriously suggest that this could be an enjoyable process—crucifixion is necessarily painful. But Paul says

---

[6] "Going Hard after the Holy God," DesiringGod, accessed December 29, 2017, http://www.desiringgod.org/sermons/going-hard-after-the-holy-god.

that if we are crucified with Christ, then we will also be raised up with Him (v. 4). In other words, there is inexpressible joy to be experienced on the other side of godly sorrow.

An Alternative Perspective on Repentance

Having addressed a few possible objections to what I consider the biblical view of repentance, I want to briefly discuss a perspective on repentance that is prevalent in the church. My intention is not to belittle this perspective but simply to identify and evaluate it using the touchstone of Scripture. Nor do I intend to pass judgment on those who hold and teach it; I am a man as prone to error as they. Nevertheless, I think it's wise to point out where they deviate from Scripture in order that we might avoid those pitfalls.

One of the most widespread views among evangelicals is expressed in *The Baker Illustrated Bible Commentary*. Its editors (Burge and Hill) argue that the Greek word for *repentance* (*metanoia*) indicates merely a "change in one's thinking."[7]

While I agree that *metanoia* does denote a change of mind, I think to limit it to that is a vast oversimplification. Are we really to believe a person can enter into eternal life by simply changing his mind about sin in the same way he might change his mind about his hairstyle or his favorite color? Clearly, we must hold to a richer and more comprehensive meaning of the word, as has been amply demonstrated already in chapter 1.

Burge and Hill also assert that repentance "connotes a willful act rather than an emotional feeling." Again, there is a grain of truth in this statement. Repentance does indeed involve an act of the will—an action that one freely chooses to do. However, the will does not act independently of the mind and the heart. Just to clarify, by the *mind*

---

[7] Gary M. Burge and Andrew E. Hill, eds., *The Baker Illustrated Bible Commentary* (Grand Rapids: Baker, 2012), 1010.

I mean the faculties of thought, reasoning, and understanding. By the *heart* I am referring to the seat of the affections or emotions, not the automatic, physiological response (e.g., sweaty palms, quickened heartbeat, butterflies in the stomach) to a stimulus such as sentimental music or an emotionally charged movie. Jonathan Edwards referred to that kind of emotional response as the stirring up of the "animal spirits."[8] Rather, the heart, as the seat of the affections, has the capacity to feel love and hatred, joy and sorrow, and desire and apathy. So, when something is called an *act of the will*, we should not think of it as something detached from the mind and heart but as something that stems from them.

Some actions are carried out primarily based on of the workings of the mind—for instance, choosing which brand of cereal to buy. A person might first make a mental calculation as to which brand is cheaper per ounce and then perform the free act of buying that brand. He may then experience a change of mind if he suddenly remembers that he has a coupon in his pocket for the other brand. Both were acts of the will based on the reasoning of the mind, or mental calculation.

The other category of actions consists of those things which are done chiefly based on the affections. This type of action occurs when a person chooses one thing over another because one appeals to him more than the other. Scripture frequently uses love/hate language to express this concept. For example, Jesus states that when a person chooses to store up money and goods rather than investing them in God's kingdom, this reveals love for money and hatred for God:

> And I say to you, make friends for yourselves by unrighteous mammon, that when you fail, they may receive you into an everlasting home. He who is faithful in what is least is faithful also in much; and he who is unjust in what is least is unjust also in much. Therefore if you have not been faithful in the unrighteous

---

[8] Jonathan Edwards, *Religious Affections* (Carlisle, PA: Banner of Truth, 1997), 59.

mammon, who will commit to your trust the true riches? And if you have not been faithful in what is another man's, who will give you what is your own?

No servant can serve two masters; for either he will hate the one and love the other, or else he will be loyal to the one and despise the other. You cannot serve God and mammon. (Luke 16:9–13)

Notice the explicit connection between practicing covetousness and the inclinations of the heart. But this concept is not confined to money. The root of lying, murder, adultery, and so on is a love for evil and hatred for righteousness (Ps. 52:3; Mic. 3:2; 1 Tim. 6:10). Thus, the impenitent sinner's foremost problem is not wrong belief or erroneous thinking but disordered affection.

If repentance were merely an act of the will, as Burge and Hill suggest, then it could be done based on mental reasoning. In this case, Judas's repentance must have been sincere; he realized how foolish he had been and changed his mind. He even went so far as to give back the money he had received for betraying Christ. Obviously, Judas did not truly repent of his sin, as we have already observed. Nowhere in Scripture is repentance for sin portrayed as the result of mere mental reasoning.

Therefore, true repentance must be an act that falls into the second category. It is born of a monumental transformation that takes place in the heart by which one begins to hate evil and love righteousness. To imply that this inward change is unnecessary—that the outward act of repentance can occur independently of the affections—is to attribute repentance (and salvation) to man, robbing God's grace of the glory which it is due.

We have seen that each of these objections, while seemingly plausible, is rooted in a misunderstanding of biblical repentance. In my experience, this confusion sometimes represents a theological blind spot, but it is more often linked to personal or relational concerns. A family member, for example, claims to have been a Christian since he was a child, yet never experienced this kind of repentance. It is easy—especially if his life shows all the trappings of Christianity—to mold our view of repentance to fit his experience. But it is vitally important that we interpret experience in the light of revelation, and not vice versa.

Chapter 4

God's Promises to the Penitent

For thus says the High and Lofty One
Who inhabits eternity, whose name is Holy:
"I dwell in the high and holy place,
With him who has a contrite and humble spirit,
To revive the spirit of the humble,
And to revive the heart of the contrite ones. (Isaiah 57:15)

In the story of Cinderella, the prince is left at the end of the night with only one token of the woman he loves: her glass slipper. He pledges to marry the woman to whom it fits and then goes far and wide searching for her. Countless women attempt to cram their foot into it (even to the point of cutting off their toes, in the original version of the story). A few can squeeze it on their foot, only to have it pop off seconds later. Each one looks at the prince expectantly, hoping that she might be the one. He, however, has no obligation to any of them, since they do not meet the condition of his promise. But when he finally finds Cinderella, and the shoe slides onto her foot, he owes it to her to ask for her hand in marriage. He loves her, of course, so this is not difficult. He joyfully keeps his promise.

This fairy tale illustrates God's obligation to the penitent. Augustine once asserted that God "has made himself our debtor, not by receiving anything from us, but by promising us all things."[1] God has pledged to set His love on the one who truly repents, so there is a sense in which God "owes" him certain things. While false penitents may, like the women in the story, wrongly presume, true penitents are provoked by this reality to sincere love, fervent prayer, and joyful hope.

Forgiveness of Sins

The first and perhaps most important of God's promises to the penitent is the forgiveness of sins: "Repent therefore and be converted, that your sins may be blotted out" (Acts 3:19). This is a beautiful promise, but we might wonder how it is connected to the truth laid out in Hebrews 9:22, that without the shedding of blood there is no forgiveness. The answer lies in the fact that repentance is essentially the act of throwing oneself at the feet of God, hoping in His mercy.

Repentance causes the sinner to seek God's provision for his sin, which is also an act of faith: "By faith Abel offered to God a more excellent sacrifice than Cain, through which he obtained witness that he was righteous" (Heb. 11:4). Similarly, penitent Old Testament saints offered sacrifices according to the Mosaic law, not trusting in their offering but in the free mercy of God. And their confidence was ultimately in God's promise to send the Messiah, who would deliver them from their sins once and for all (Gen. 3:15).

Yet there were also many Jews who remained impenitent and hardhearted, even while they offered the prescribed sacrifices, and thus they received no mercy from God. He was not interested in the sacrifice for its own sake but as a display of a heart conformed to His

---

[1] Quoted in John Calvin, *Institutes of the Christian Religion*, trans. Henry Beveridge (Grand Rapids: Eerdmans, 1997), 3:126.

own heart. God confirmed this when He told the people, "I desire mercy and not sacrifice" (Hos. 6:6).

The sacrifices of the impenitent accomplished nothing because God's mercy cannot be appropriated mechanically or by ritual. Blood was necessary for atonement, but it did not guarantee it. The high priest would enter the holy of holies once per year to make atonement for the sins of the people, but this does not mean that everyone's sins were forgiven. Only those people who appropriated God's forgiveness for themselves in repentance and faith were forgiven.

The New Testament also makes it clear that God's provision for sin is appropriated only by the penitent. When the Pharisees criticized Jesus for eating with tax collectors and sinners, He responded: "Those who are well have no need of a physician, but those who are sick. But go and learn what this means: 'I desire mercy and not sacrifice.' For I did not come to call the righteous, but sinners, to repentance" (Matt. 9:12–13).

The word *for* at the beginning of verse 13 is significant because it connects Jesus's quotation of Hosea 6:6 to the Pharisee's inability to come to Him as sick people to a physician. Jesus was pointing them to the essence of Hosea's words—namely, that God desires inward conformity to Himself and not mere outward obedience. He told them to go and meditate on their lack of conformity to God's heart (displayed in their lack of mercy) until they were ready to approach the Great Physician as desperate, miserable sinners. Only then would they be ready to take hold of God's provision for their sins.

God's promise of forgiveness of sins is reiterated in 1 John 1:9: "If we confess our sins, He is faithful and just to forgive us our sins and to cleanse us from all unrighteousness." Here we learn that both God's faithfulness and justice are displayed in His forgiveness of the penitent. His faithfulness is exhibited in that He is keeping His promise to forgive the penitent's sins. The true penitent can be certain that God has forgiven his sins. God's justice is demonstrated in forgiveness because He has already judged the penitent's sin in the person of Jesus Christ. Matthew Henry insightfully expands on this truth:

> He is just to himself and his glory who has provided such a sacrifice, by which his righteousness is declared in the justification of sinners. He is just to his Son who has not only sent him for such service, but promised to him that those who come through him shall be forgiven on his account. "By his knowledge (by the believing apprehension of him) shall my righteous servant justify many" (Is. 53:11). He is clement and gracious also, and so will forgive, to the contrite confessor, all his sins.[2]

Cleansing from All Unrighteousness

Forgiveness of sins is not the only promise to the penitent in 1 John 1:9. They are also promised that God will cleanse them from all unrighteousness. These two promises are inextricably linked. This connection might be illustrated by Jesus's calming of the storm. We read in Mark 4:39 that Jesus "arose and rebuked the wind, and said to the sea, 'Peace, be still!' And the wind ceased and there was a great calm." Not only did Jesus eliminate the immediate cause of their trouble (the waves), but He also removed the root cause. Both occurred simultaneously.

Similarly, the penitent sinner not only has the guilt of his sins removed, but he also is cleansed from unrighteousness—the root of the problem. While he is not free from sin, there has been a decisive break from it in his heart; its power over him has been broken. In Paul's letter to the Corinthians, he lists the kinds of people who will not enter God's kingdom, such as fornicators, homosexuals, and

---

[2] Matthew Henry, *Matthew Henry's Commentary on the Whole Bible* (Peabody, MA: Hendrickson, 1996), 2,443.

idolaters. Then he writes, "And such *were* some of you" (1 Cor. 6:11, emphasis mine). In other words, since repenting of these sins, they have been cleansed from the power of unrighteousness. They are no longer slaves to it (to use Paul's wording in Rom. 6). Now they are free to live for God.

Nearness to God

Another precious promise that God makes to the penitent is intimacy with Himself. David writes, "The LORD is near to those who have a broken heart, and saves such as have a contrite spirit" (Ps. 34:18). Like a mother tenderly wraps her arms around her grieving child, drawing him near, the Father embraces the brokenhearted sinner. Concerning this promise, John Gill writes:

> [The brokenhearted are those] with a sense of sin, and sorrow for it, for which their hearts smite them, and they are wounded by it, and broken with it: to these the Lord is "nigh"; not in a general way only, as he is to all men, being God omnipresent, but in a special manner; he comes and manifests himself to them in a gracious way, pours in the oil and wine of his love, and binds up their broken hearts; yea, comes and dwells with them. . . . He heals their breaches.[3]

This promise is also embedded in the parable of the prodigal son. Rather than waiting for his penitent son to walk to him, the father ran to him, threw his arms around him, and kissed him. It would have been more than generous for the father to allow this young man to become like one of his hired servants, who probably lived in separate quarters. But he does much more than that; he welcomes him back into his home as a son. The tragic irony is that the elder son, proud and self-righteous, is the one left standing outside the father's house (albeit by his own choice). This brings to mind Psalm 138:6, which

---

[3] "John Gill's Exposition of the Whole Bible: Psalms 34," Studylight.org, accessed January 2, 2018, https://www.studylight.org/commentaries/geb/psalms-34.html.

reveals the other side of the promise: "Though the LORD is on high, yet He regards the lowly; but the proud He knows from afar." While God draws near to the penitent, He cannot bear to have the impenitent in His presence. And, like the proud son in the parable, they don't want to be near Him.

The question for each of us, to revisit the metaphor at the beginning of the chapter, is *does the shoe fit?* If it does, then we can take great comfort in knowing God has kept, and will keep, His promises to forgive our sins, cleanse our unrighteousness, and draw us near to Himself.

Chapter 5

Implications for Evangelism

*And that repentance and remission of sins should be preached
in His name to all nations, beginning at Jerusalem. (Luke 24:47)*

One of the unique aspects of Christianity is the way in which it
spreads. Some of the world's religions advance by the sword, and
others by the teaching of a philosophy. But the living God has
ordained that His kingdom would be advanced by the proclamation
of the message of the gospel, the *evangelion*.

Whenever this message is faithfully proclaimed with the intent of
leading people to God through Jesus Christ, evangelism occurs. A
right understanding of repentance is essential to the faithful
proclamation of the gospel and therefore has tremendous
implications for the way in which evangelism is conducted. These
implications can be divided into five main categories: the basis for
evangelism, preparation for evangelism, the method of evangelism,
the message of the evangelist, and expectations for evangelism.

The Basis for Evangelism

I'll begin with the basis for evangelism, which would seem to be the
same regardless of how one views repentance—namely, a love for
souls and a burning desire to bring them to Jesus Christ. This is

certainly true, but there are some subtle differences in the underlying motivations for winning souls, which turn out to be of tremendous importance. The person who has not experienced true repentance or does not have a right understanding of it may evangelize, even effectively (Phil. 1:15–18). But his evangelism will likely be driven by altruism, sentimental humanism, personality, a sense of duty, or selfish ambition rather than love for God. For it is in repentance that one sees how much he needs to be forgiven of, and then he receives that forgiveness through faith in Christ. Because he is forgiven much, he loves much (Luke 7:47), thus fulfilling the first command to love God with all his heart, soul, mind, and strength (Luke 10:27). Only on the basis of this all-consuming love for God can he fulfill the second command to love his neighbor as himself (Luke 10:27), which is to say that he sincerely desires his neighbor's eternal salvation and happiness. This desire is not for the sake of his neighbor primarily but for the sake of God's glory, which is magnificently displayed when God imparts grace to a depraved rebel and makes him a son, an heir of the glorious inheritance that is the kingdom of God.

Furthermore, it is the uniform testimony of Scripture that God saves men for the sake of His praise, glory, honor, and renown (1 Sam. 12:22; Ps. 23:3; 79:9; Rom. 9:17, 22–23). To the unregenerate, this seems self-serving and egotistical, but not so for those who have tasted the glory of His grace. For them, His praise, glory, honor, and renown become their sweetest delight and highest aim, and their hearts are aflame with passion for advancing the gospel. They know what it means to "seek first the kingdom of God" (Matt. 6:33) and can say with Paul, "But none of these things move me; nor do I count my life dear to myself, so that I may finish my race with joy, and the ministry which I received from the Lord Jesus, to testify to the gospel of the grace of God" (Acts 20:24). Thus, repentance is requisite to loving God and others and desiring His kingdom, and these are the basis for evangelism.

Preparation for Evangelism

Next, let us examine the way in which a right view of repentance shapes our preparation for evangelism. Few would disagree with the assertion that prayer is vital to effective evangelism. However, the evangelist who understands repentance knows it is not his responsibility but God's to bring men to repentance and faith. He knows that the success of his efforts is utterly dependent on God and therefore invests much time and energy in prayer. What is the proper subject of his prayer? First, he will obey Jesus's command to "pray the Lord of the harvest to send out laborers into His harvest" (Luke 10:2).

But some might object, why pray if God has already chosen those whom He is going to save and will certainly bring them to repentance and faith? First, it is a command of Christ and therefore ought to be done with all diligence by those who call Him Lord and Master. Second, we must recognize that God uses the means He has appointed to bring people to salvation—sending workers into the field. He does this by putting an irresistible desire in people's hearts to go out and preach the gospel to lost souls. But won't He do this even if I don't pray? Absolutely. But if I have no urge to pray for this, then I am not about my Master's business and ought to seriously question whether I am truly God's servant.

To further understand the basis for and importance of prayer in evangelism, consider the prayer of Elijah the prophet. James tells us: "Elijah was a man with a nature like ours, and he prayed earnestly that it would not rain; and it did not rain on the land for three years and six months. And he prayed again, and the heaven gave rain, and the earth produced its fruit" (James 5:17–18).

The account to which James here refers is found in chapters 17 and 18 of 1 Kings. God had sovereignly chosen to punish the people of Israel for their idolatry by withholding rain, thereby causing a famine. God might have accomplished this by simply speaking a word (or without any means at all), but instead, He put it into Elijah's heart to pray for it and granted his request. Then, after three and a half years of drought, God told Elijah that He was going to send rain. Elijah might have sat back and waited for God to act, but he did no such thing. Rather, he hiked to the top of Mount Carmel, fell on his face before God, and prayed for rain. And he didn't just pray once and get back to his daily routine, satisfied he had done his duty. He prayed seven times before he finally saw the cloud approaching that would end Israel's famine.

Make no mistake; God uses means to bring souls into His kingdom, just like He used means to withhold rain and to send it forth in Israel. God wants us to pray that He will send workers into the field as well as that He will make their (and our own) labor effective. And realizing that repentance is nothing less than a miracle wrought by the Holy Spirit in the heart, we should pray that God will grant our hearers repentance (2 Tim. 2:25) and cause "the light of the knowledge of the glory of God in the face of Jesus Christ" to shine into their hearts (2 Cor. 4:6). We must have an unshakable confidence He is able to accomplish this and that He has appointed prayer-supported evangelism to do so.

It should therefore come as no surprise that prayer has preceded every true revival in the history of the church. Evangelist Duncan Campbell defined revival as the occasion when

> the community suddenly becomes conscious of the movings of God, beginning with His own people. So that, in a matter of hours, (not days), . . . churches become crowded. No information of any special meeting, but something happening that moves men and women to a house of God, and you'll find within hours, scores of men and women crying to God for mercy.[1]

---

[1] Duncan Campbell, "When God Stepped Down," accessed June 19, 2018, https://media.sermonaudio.com/mediapdf/91088123510.pdf

The first example of such an event is found in the second chapter of Acts, beginning on the day of Pentecost. Virtually all Christians can identify this as the day marked by the unprecedented outpouring of the Spirit of God. But the activity of the disciples in the ten days immediately following Christ's ascension and prior to Pentecost often goes unnoticed, namely that "they continually devoted themselves to prayer" (Acts 1:14, NASB). While Luke does not tell us the content of their prayers, it is reasonable to infer that it was related to Jesus's promise that they would be filled and empowered by the Holy Spirit to bring the gospel to the ends of the earth (Acts 1:8). After a week and a half of constant prayer, God responded. On the Jewish feast of Pentecost, the Spirit filled the disciples, which attracted a crowd of Jews. Peter preached the gospel to them, and the Spirit convicted them of their sin: "Now when they heard this, they were cut to the heart, and said to Peter and the rest of the apostles, 'Men and brethren, what shall we do?'" (Acts 2:37). They subsequently believed on Jesus and were baptized. On that day alone, three thousand men repented and believed, and many more would be added to that number in the days to come.

God imparts to a group of believers the fervent desire for the salvation of souls, they pray accordingly, He pours out His Spirit, and people hear the gospel and are saved. This was true of the Pentecost revival, and it has been a common theme among revivals ever since.

The First Great Awakening, an eighteenth-century revival in the American colonies, was preceded by the fervent prayers of ministers like Jonathan Edwards and George Whitefield as well as lesser-known Theodore Frelinghuysen, the pastor of a Dutch Reformed congregation in New Jersey. These ministers, along with others, recognized the desperate spiritual condition of their people and prayed that God would do a great work in them. God heard this prayer, and beginning around 1733, a spiritual awakening swept through the colonies, in which, according to Edwards, "It was a very frequent thing to see a houseful of outcries, faintings, convulsions, and suchlike, both with distress (over sin) and also with admiration and joy."[2] This extraordinary work of the Spirit lasted well into the 1750s, leaving in its wake hundreds of thousands of regenerated souls and transforming the spiritual and moral climate of the colonies. Subsequent American revivals, such as the Second Great Awakening, which took place about fifty years later, and the New York City revival of 1857, followed a similar pattern.

I would be remiss if I did not mention the revival that took place on the Isle of Lewis, an island off the coast of Scotland. It began in the 1940s when two elderly women and some of the leaders from their church began to pray two nights each week, all through the night, that God would bring many in their town to salvation. These prayer meetings continued for weeks until God began to do a marvelous work, not only in that town but throughout the entire island.

Evangelist Duncan Campbell, through whom God worked for three years in Lewis, said that one of the primary features of this revival was the "deep, deep conviction of sin."[3] One of the most striking examples of this was an old farmer named Donald McCloud. Donald's wife convinced him to go to church one evening, but he had to sit on the steps because the church was full. While he was sitting there, the Spirit of God convicted him of sin, and he began crying out, "Hell is too good for me! Hell is too good for me!" After he had continued in this state for some time, Campbell visited him in his room and found him on his knees, repeating, "God, can You have mercy on me?" The next morning, Donald received an answer to that question as he encountered the mercy of God in the person of Christ and surrendered his life to Him. Donald was one of the many thousands

---

[2] Jonathan Edwards, *Jonathan Edwards on Revival* (Carlisle, PA: Banner of Truth, 2014), 151.

[3] Campbell, "When God Stepped Down."

to whom God granted salvation during this revival, thus honoring the holy longing and fervent prayers of a few faithful saints.

The Method of Evangelism

The next facet of evangelism which is affected by a biblical view of repentance is the method in which we conduct evangelism. It is important to understand there is no command in Scripture to follow a certain method when preaching the gospel of Christ. Therefore, the formats we use may be as varied as the setting in which Christ is preached. Personal, one-on-one evangelism will take on different forms as will evangelism carried out within the walls of the church, on the streets, and in the stadium. In this sense, method will largely be determined by circumstances. Nevertheless, the person who rightly understands repentance will take a decidedly different approach than the one who does not. I am not here speaking of repentance to the exclusion of faith but assuming the two are coupled together.

First, the one who understands repentance is a *sovereign* work of God and that He gives it to whomever He will does not place undue emphasis on methods. By this I do not mean that one ought to put no thought into methods at all, for we have seen that God often uses means. Rather, I am asserting that instead of researching trends in modern evangelism and planning sophisticated outreaches, he spends most of his time preparing his own heart and equipping his mind by meditating on God's Word, pleading with God for the souls of those he will evangelize, and doing evangelism.

Second, the one who understands that repentance is a *holy* work of God will not use deceptive, worldly, or covert schemes for sharing Christ. One example of this kind of method that comes to mind is an evangelistic outreach I helped with in conjunction with the campus ministry at the secular college I attended. We started planning the event several months out and decided that we would stir up curiosity and interest among the student body by having everyone from our group wear bright orange t-shirts that read "I Agree with Tom. Do You Agree with Tom?" (Tom was the ministry leader who would be preaching.) Then in smaller letters below, it gave the details of the event. When I wore my shirt to my creative writing class one morning, a few of my classmates commented about how many people they had seen wearing those shirts. The professor took note, and as he was about to begin his lecture, he looked me in the eyes and made a remark that profoundly affected me. He said, "You know, John, you can't trick people into the kingdom."

There are a host of other examples of profane evangelistic methods used today by well-meaning people, from giving out movie tickets to holding mixed martial arts tournaments in the church building. One major problem with these is succinctly stated by Paul Washer: "If you use carnal means to attract men, you're going to attract carnal men, and you're going to have to keep using greater carnal means to keep them in the church."[4]

But there is an even greater danger than this in using illegitimate methods—namely that "the cross of Christ should be made of no effect" (1 Cor. 1:17). The method that would have this outcome, according to this verse, is preaching the gospel "with wisdom of words"—that is, the oratorical skill and precision of philosophical language that the Greeks valued so highly. Notice that Paul is asserting that this method of evangelizing would render the preaching of the cross futile, even if the content of the message were the true gospel. I would argue that some of the methods being used today, while perhaps not the wisdom of words, are still rooted in the wisdom of the world and are thus very dangerous, no matter how well they seem to work. "For the wisdom of this world is foolishness with

---

[4] *Divided*, directed by Leclerc Brothers (St. Chicopee, MA: Leclerc Brothers Motion Pictures, 2010), DVD.

God. For it is written, 'He catches the wise in their own craftiness'" (1 Cor. 3:19).

Some might object that these methods are simply designed to bring people in to hear the preaching of the gospel and do not affect the message itself. This argument sounds plausible, but the reality is that those who use these methods often present a gospel message that is as shallow and man-centered as the means used to attract people. For to present the true gospel to a man after luring him in with carnal means would be the equivalent of dipping a stick of tofu in chocolate, wrapping it in a candy wrapper, and giving it to some unsuspecting little boy. He will undoubtedly be excited to receive the treat, but after taking one bite of it, he will throw it on the ground and never accept anything from you again.

If a Christian wants to preach the gospel but is worried that no one will come to hear him, let him go to them. He ought to go to the streets, college campuses, people's houses, open mic night at the local café, or wherever else there are lost souls. Paul never held a massive crusade in the Coliseum, but I doubt anyone has won more souls to Christ than he. It's not that large-scale outreaches are an inherently corrupt method, but if one needs to use worldly means to lure people to attend, then he'd best avoid them.

Third, the one who understands repentance is the *sole* work of God does not use methods that tend to exalt the will and actions of individuals over the working of God. In this category I would place such practices as the altar call (along with the playing of emotionally manipulative music that often accompanies it); the planting of church members in the audience who, when the invitation is given, come forward in order to encourage those who are hesitant to come; and the reciting of the "Sinner's Prayer." Such methods are unscriptural and are rooted ultimately in natural religion, the essence of which is seen in the attempt by Adam and Eve to make for themselves coverings out of fig leaves. They knew that sin had marred their souls and alienated them from God, so they set out, with characteristic ingenuity, to do something about it. We might wonder how they came to think that foliage was God's approved means of covering their nakedness, but I suppose it was simply what they had at their disposal.

Similarly, when a man attends a church service or evangelistic crusade and receives confirmation of what he already suspected—that he is a sinner and his sin has separated him from God—his conscience may be awakened or disturbed. Of course, this is not comfortable, so he becomes very receptive to any suggestion as to how he might find relief. When he hears the preacher tell him to come to the altar or raise his hand and repeat a prayer, he is more than happy to comply. But in doing so, he is simply following the pattern established by Adam, covering his shame with the fig leaf of human effort. American evangelist Lewis S. Chafer (who at one time used and advocated these methods) understood this problem well and aptly stated it as follows:

> Because of satanic blindness to the Gospel of Grace (2 Cor 4:3–4), unregenerate man cannot comprehend the true basis of salvation, and is therefore ever prone to do the best he knows. This is to attempt to work out his own standing before God by his own efforts. It is this natural tendency to do something of merit that prompts many to respond to the evangelist's appeal. ... A leader with a commanding personality (and every successful evangelist must possess that characteristic in the extreme) may secure the public action of many, when the issue is made one of religious merit through some public act. Under such an impression, a serious person may stand in a meeting who has no conception of what is involved in standing by faith on the Rock Christ Jesus; or he may be persuaded to abandon his natural

timidity when he knows nothing of abandoning his satanic tendency to self-help.[5]

Repentance in the Modern Invitation System

One of the defining marks of modern mass evangelism is the "invitation" that is offered at the end of the message. This usually includes a call for those who want to receive Christ to come to the front of the room or to raise their hand. They are then encouraged to repeat a prayer after the evangelist, speak with a counselor, and fill out a card so that someone can follow up with them. From a pragmatic perspective, this method ought to be used without hesitation by any evangelist who wants to see converts, as it has led to hundreds of millions—perhaps billions—of "decisions for Christ" since its inception two centuries ago. But from a biblical and theological perspective the invitation system (the system that embraces these methods) is highly problematic, as it has led to the distorted view of repentance that pervades evangelicalism today.

As has already been noted, true repentance requires a sovereign, saving work of the Holy Spirit in a person's heart whereby he begins to see his sin for what it is, grieve over it, hate it, experience shame for it, confess it, and turn from it. The first four of these represent a turning of the heart against sin, while the last two represent a turning away from sin in word and deed. Change of behavior must be rooted in change of heart. Unregenerate man can—and often does—turn away from particular sins out of self-interest, pride, or guilt. This self-reformation may even result from hearing the gospel. Iain Murray argues:

> We may even go further, with Scripture, and say that where the truth is preached there will be a general kind of conviction wrought by the Spirit which disturbs men's consciences and

---

[5] Lewis S. Chafer, quoted in Iain H. Murray, *The Invitation System* (Carlisle: Banner of Truth Trust, 2002), 23.

makes them willing to look for some relief . . . [and unless they are born again] they will proceed to act on that principle which lies at the root of all natural religion, the belief that *man can do something to put himself right with God.*"[6]

It is exactly this kind of self-help that is encouraged by modern evangelists. They portray repentance as assenting to the reality of sin and its consequences, asking God's forgiveness, and committing to turn from sin. Billy Graham, for example, called on his hearers to "acknowledge that you've failed God, that you've sinned against God, and [be] willing to renounce your sins and to give up your sins."[7] Similarly, Greg Laurie tells unbelievers, "You must admit that you are a sinner . . . and walk away from sin and toward Christ."[8] Luis Palau asserts, "Repentance is the biblical, correct response to sin. God's Word, the Bible, teaches that, first, we must admit our sins have separated us from God and, second, we must believe what Christ has done for us on the cross."[9]

While there is an element of truth in these exhortations, they amount to nothing more than an appeal to unregenerate sinners to do what they can to cover their own nakedness. It requires nothing outside of man's natural resources to acknowledge he is a sinner and that his sin separates him from God. Many, if not most, unbelievers have a nagging sense of guilt resulting from violations of conscience. When they are offered hope by an evangelist that this burden can be lifted simply by admitting what they already knew to be true and assenting to certain propositions about Jesus, many will take him up on his

---

[6] Murray, *The Invitation System*, 21.

[7] "Billy Graham: What is Repentance?" YouTube, accessed January 2, 2018, https://youtu.be/irRjydQYVVY.

[8] "Whatever Happened to the Clear Invitation?" *Christianity Today*, accessed January 2, 2018, http://www.christianitytoday.com/pastors/1995/spring/ 5l2052.html.

[9] "Hope for Healing," Luis Palau Association, accessed June 19, 2018, http://legacy.palau.org/resources/articles/spiritual-growth/item/hope-for-healing.

offer. But they remain in their sin, and unless God grants them true repentance, they will die in it. It might be argued, however, that this is true of all evangelism, regardless of the method. Indeed, in Matthew 13:47–50, Jesus likens the kingdom of heaven to a large fishing net that fisherman have thrown into the water. When the time comes to drag it to shore, it has caught all kinds of fish—some "good" and some "corrupt." The good are put into containers, and the bad are thrown away. Jesus then interprets the parable for His disciples, explaining that this is how it will be at the judgment, when people are sorted and the wicked are cast into hell.

We know that whenever the gospel is preached, all kinds are going to be drawn. And like the wheat and the tares, they will be together and largely indistinguishable from one another. But in the end, many of them will be found to be corrupt and will be cast into hell. This is unavoidable because of the nature of the gospel; it is a beautiful message, and for this reason it attracts all kinds of people, including those who remain impenitent and faithless. But while the reprobate have always been drawn into the net along with the elect, it seems that over the last two centuries we have been precision-engineering our net to catch bad fish. That is, we have designed a gospel presentation that seems calculated to bring false converts into the church and to cultivate self-deception. Albert Dod correctly affirms, "Had this system been designed to lead the sinner . . . to self-deception, in what important respect could it have been better adapted than it now is to this purpose?"[10]

This is not to say that true repentance cannot take place within the invitation system; the Holy Spirit works in ways we would not expect. But He is the Spirit of truth (John 14:17), and therefore, it is usually through the proclamation of truth and the call to true repentance that

---

[10] Albert B. Dod, *Essays: Theological and Miscellaneous* (New York: Wiley and Putnam, 1847), 129

He operates. Therefore, I believe that it is despite the invitation system, and not directly through it, that He works repentance in the hearts of the elect who attend such meetings.

To understand the distortion of the doctrine of repentance in modern evangelism, it is necessary to trace it back to its roots. Prior to the entrance of Charles G. Finney into the field of evangelism early in the nineteenth century, the invitation system (the system that makes use of altar calls, the Sinner's Prayer, etc.) was unknown to Christianity. Finney did not believe in the doctrine of original sin in the traditional sense (that is, that we inherit Adam's sinful *nature*). Rather, he believed we follow Adam's sinful *example*. So, when he called on his hearers to repent, what he meant was, *transform your life so that it more closely aligns with Christ's.* He emphasized the necessity of "submitting to Christ," which, as Dod notes, is a theologically significant phrase:

> We are at no loss to understand why Mr. Finney presents the sinner's duty in this form. Submission seems to be more comprised than some other duties within a single mental act, and more capable of instant performance. Were the sinner directed to repent, it might seem to imply that he should take some little time to think of his sins, and of the Being whom he has offended. . . . Repentance . . . therefore, will not so well answer his purpose. But with submission, he can move the sinner to the instant performance of the duty involved.[11]

One of the methods Finney pioneered was the "anxious seat," which was basically the prototype of the modern altar call. He believed that by coming to the anxious seat after the message to speak with the minister and pray, the person's decision to follow Christ would be reinforced, and he would thus be less likely to fall away. It was this public act that sealed the deal, so to speak. Later this technique would

---

[11] Dod, 128.

incorporate the Sinner's Prayer, a standardized prayer which those who went forward would recite to become a Christian.

Finney's methods seemed to work; hundreds of thousands attended his crusades and made a profession of faith. But a short time after his crusades ended, vast regions where "revival" had swept through became known as the "burned-over districts," because the supposed converts had lapsed back into their former ways. Unfortunately, many people today have not only embraced the methods that Finney pioneered but are unaware that evangelism was ever practiced without them. Finney's theological offspring continue to call on sinners to turn away from their sins without necessarily having any real aversion to them in their heart.

Regrettably, it is not only the preaching of mass evangelists that has conveyed a distorted view of repentance; it has also occurred through "gospel" tracts such as the *Four Spiritual Laws* and *3 Circles*. In these, every aspect of the gospel message undergoes a subtle shift. The ultimate aim of salvation shifts from "the praise of the glory of His grace" (Eph. 1:6) to attaining God's "wonderful plan for your life."[12] The definition of sin naturally changes from rebellion against God to "stubborn self-will"[13] (not going along with this wonderful plan). The problem with sin is that it is the primary obstacle to man's happiness and personal fulfillment. Broken-heartedness over sin becomes the pain and frustration that we feel when "life is not working."[14] Repentance, then, transforms into the acknowledgment that "we don't have the power to escape this brokenness on our own" and the

---

[12] Bill Bright, "Have You Heard of the Four Spiritual Laws?" accessed December 9, 2018, http://www.4laws.com/laws/englishkgp/default.htm.
[13] "Four Spiritual Laws."
[14] North American Mission Board, "3 Circles: Life Conversation Guide," Life on Mission, accessed December 9, 2018, http://lifeonmissionbook.com/conversation-guide.

act of "ask[ing] God to forgive us."[15] Finally, the good news itself becomes Christ dying to give us a "full and meaningful" life.[16] Nowhere do these tracts warn the sinner that he has violated God's laws, he is living in rebellion against God, and consequently, God's wrath abides on him (John 3:36).

While there are elements of truth in these tracts, I believe they convey a fundamentally different view of repentance, and ultimately, a different gospel. The sinner's primary problem is not a lack of meaning or personal fulfillment, though these are certainly by-products of sin. Rather, man's real predicament is that his sin—both the innate corruption of his heart and actual sins committed—sets him at enmity against his holy and righteous Creator. When this truth is set forth as the basis for repentance, and the Holy Spirit confirms it through His work of conviction, the sinner cries out with Isaiah, "Woe is me, for I am undone!" (Isa. 6:5). Now he is ready to be made whole by Christ.

Before proceeding further, I want to briefly address the use of visual media as an evangelistic tool. This might include *The Jesus Film*, gospel tracts with depictions of Jesus, or a live dramatic presentation of the gospel. While these methods are used by many well-meaning Christians with seemingly positive results, we must remember that true Christianity is thoroughly propositional; it is a faith centered around the *Word*, not the image. Christians are a people of the Book. This is one aspect of the faith that we inherited from the Jews, to whom God commanded, "You shall not make for yourself a carved image—any likeness of anything that is in heaven above, or that is in the earth beneath, or that is in the water under the earth" (Deut. 5:8).

And Christ is referred to in John 1:1 as "the Word," which among other things, means that those who will receive Him must do so with

---

[15] "3 Circles."

[16] "Four Spiritual Laws."

divinely enlightened *understanding*, not by physical sight (Acts 26:18). In fact, faith is pitted against sight in 2 Corinthians 5:7, which states that "we walk by faith, not by sight." Watching a series of images moving on a screen does nothing to help us to see Christ in the way we need to, which is through the eyes of faith. Visual media can certainly stir the emotions, but not in a way that will bring a man any closer to true repentance and faith.

I don't mean to imply that no one has ever been brought to salvation through these questionable methods, but if they have been, it was despite them, not because of them. Let the one who wants to win souls do so in the divinely appointed method of *preaching*, and let the message be "repentance and remission of sins . . . in His name" (Luke 27:47).

This must be the message of the evangelist, but there are some things that he must also convey that will give meaning to it. His hearers must first understand that God created mankind in His own image and for His purposes, including the joyous beholding, reflecting, enjoying, and praising of His glory (Rom. 1:21). Confirming the necessity of this aspect of gospel preaching, J. I. Packer states, "The gospel starts by teaching that we, as creatures, are absolutely dependent upon God, and he, as Creator, has an absolute claim on us. Only when we have learned this can we see what sin is."[17]

For it is in the light of God's perfect design and total authority over His creation that it is possible to see we are fallen creatures, alienated from Him by the nature which we have inherited from Adam (Rom. 5:12). The doctrine of a corrupt and sinful nature provides the basis for understanding why everything unregenerate man does, even his most benevolent actions, is sin in God's sight. Out of his corrupt

---

[17] J. I. Packer, *Evangelism and the Sovereignty of God* (Downers Grove, IL: Intervarsity Press, 2008), 61.

nature spring corrupt actions, or to paraphrase Jesus, from a bad tree comes bad fruit (Matt. 7:17).

The Right Use of the Law

But for the sinner to have a general understanding that we are all sinful is not enough. He must be brought to see the extent of his own corruption and the wickedness of his personal sins. I want to emphasize here the fact that this is the work of the Spirit of God and not of man. Nevertheless, God has given us His law as a tool for this purpose. In fact, Paul calls it our "tutor" or "schoolmaster" (KJV) "to bring us to Christ" (Gal. 3:24). Therefore, if a Christian seeks to lead someone to Christ, he should start with the account of creation in Genesis, and then take his listener to the Ten Commandments in Exodus 20. This accomplishes two things. First, he will see the perfections of God's nature and character more clearly and explicitly than they can be seen in creation. For example, we see God's worthiness of our worship and jealousy for it (v. 3); His holiness and the honor of His name (v. 7); His intrinsic authority and ability to bestow it on humans (v. 12); His generosity in giving and preserving life, marriage, and property (vv. 13–15); and His truthfulness (v. 16). In the light of the excellence of God's nature, he may see the corruptions of his own.

Further, in the Ten Commandments, the sinner sees God's righteous and unchanging standard, which he is constantly violating through his wicked thoughts, words, and actions. "By the law is the knowledge of sin," Paul states in Romans 3:20. For some, their sins are so egregious they have no problem coming to the knowledge of sin. Perhaps they have practiced the occult or taken the life of another or been caught in an adulterous affair. But for many, especially those who have been raised up in good families and have been "churched," their sins are subtler and provide a sort of safe-haven of self-righteousness in which they can hide from the light of the law. When sharing with this type of individual, the evangelist must be sure to assail their fortress with the spirit of the law, the essence of the Ten Commandments, as Jesus did with the Pharisees. He acknowledged they knew and outwardly obeyed God's prohibitions against murder and adultery. But He demonstrated they had murder and adultery in their hearts, in that they showed contempt to their fellow man and gazed lustfully at women. The sound evangelist must follow Jesus's example in this.

I was sharing the gospel with a young man in my church who had professed faith but showed little evidence of true repentance. I asked him, "William (not his real name), do you think that you deserve hell?" He replied that he did not. I asked, "Do you think that God would be right to send to hell a person who disobeys just one of His commandments?" To this he replied in the affirmative. I then asked William if he had ever worshiped idols, to which he responded with an emphatic "No!"

"Are there things in your life to which you've given your heart—things that, when you think about them, you get more of a sense of delight than when you think about God and that you enjoy doing more than spending time with God?"

"Well, yes," he replied with hesitation.

"Then you are an idol worshiper, William."

I proceeded to go through a few more of the commandments with him in the same manner. "You told me that God would be just in condemning a person to eternal judgment who had broken one of God's commands. And you have violated just about the whole law of God. Do you see that you stand before God as a sinner, deserving of a thousand eternities in hell?"

At this point, William's eyes began to tear up, and he said "Yes, I see that." I went on.

"You sin because you have a corrupt nature; your heart is full of evil. The Bible tells us that God is too pure to look at sin (Hab. 1:13), so if you were to die and stand before His righteous eyes, you would melt like a wax figure in a furnace. But even right now, God's wrath is on you."

William was pretty upset by this point, and I felt like this might be the beginnings of conviction. So I proceeded to tell him about Christ being given as a sacrifice so that, for the one who believes on Him, God's wrath is transferred from him to Christ on the cross, and Christ's perfect righteousness is transferred to the believer. I then prayed for William that God would continue to open his eyes to see his sin, turn him against it in his heart and away from it in his life, and that Christ would become great and precious to him, that he might flee to Christ.

I do not provide this anecdote as a model of effective evangelism but only to illustrate the fact that the law exposes sin in those who are righteous in their own eyes. It is by the power of the Spirit and the Word of God that this knowledge of sin is driven into the sinner's heart, bringing him to repentance.

However, the evangelist must not only preach the law with his mouth but also with his actions. His life ought to be ever-increasingly conformed to God's law, since the Spirit of the God who gave the commandments is living in him. This internal resonance with the law preaches powerfully and is a great help in bringing someone to the consciousness of sin. The Philippian jailer (Acts 16) was brought under great distress of soul through the witness of Paul and Silas. Their upright character and piety as they sang hymns to God was a living testimony of the law of God. The Spirit used the temporal personal crisis of prisoners escaping to bring his sin and spiritual helplessness to the forefront, causing the jailer to run to them, fall down trembling, and cry out, "Sirs, what must I do to be saved?" (v. 30). The combination of consciousness of sin and the onset of desperate circumstances is often used by the Spirit to bring a person to repentance (Gen. 42:21; Ps. 107). With this in mind, let the evangelist preach the law in both word and deed in order to make men conscious of their sin, that his hearers will be prepared to receive Christ. For the grace of God in Christ only makes sense when presented in the context of the just judgment and wrath of the holy, righteous God toward those who have offended Him. Then, not only does grace make sense, but it appears exceedingly precious.

After the soil of the heart has been plowed with the law of God and prepared in penitence by the Holy Spirit, it is ready for the seed of the gospel of Jesus Christ. Or to put it another way, when the patient has been made to comprehend the severity of his sickness, he is ready to receive the good news that the cure is to be found in Jesus Christ. And the evangelist must present the Great Physician in all His glory—His eternal Godhead, humble incarnation, sinless perfection, active obedience, inexhaustible mercy and love, atoning death on the cross, bodily resurrection, ascension into heaven, eternal glory, and imminent return. Let the evangelist magnify the glory of God's grace toward sinners in Christ, by which God reconciles wicked rebels to Himself so that He may bestow upon them a glorious inheritance in His Son.

The penitent sinner does not need to hear that his felt needs—those things he believes to be necessary for his personal happiness—will be met by Christ; this will only be a distraction to him. Thus, the evangelist who understands repentance will necessarily shun common expressions such as "God has a wonderful plan for your life" and "There's a void in your heart, and only God can fill it," along with all promises of a better life, a saved marriage, or earthly happiness. For if the sinner understands his need correctly, his primary concern is to be reconciled to the God he has so grievously offended by taking hold of Christ with every fiber of his being. Pandering to self-love will only attract the impenitent to an imaginary, Santa Claus-like savior, whom they will desert in trouble, leaving their hearts inoculated against the true Christ.

Expectations

The final thing I want to address concerning the impact of biblical repentance on evangelism is our expectations for evangelism. The sound evangelist expects God will grant some repentance through his ministry. He knows "God ... commands all men everywhere to repent" (Acts 17:30) and that God is faithful to grant what He commands. When Christ commanded Lazarus to come out of the tomb, bound up in that command was the power required for him to obey. The gospel preacher therefore expects that, as he sounds forth this command of God, some will heed that call and enter into eternal life. When Paul was in Corinth, God exhorted him to continue preaching by telling him, "Do not be afraid, but speak, and do not keep silent . . . for I have many people in this city" (Acts 18:10). Paul's expectation for his own safety and the effectiveness of His preaching came from the knowledge that some of those to whom he would be preaching were among the elect and that God would certainly grant them repentance and faith by means of his preaching. God may not give that specific encouragement to every evangelist, but He doesn't need to, for we know His word is "living and powerful" (Heb. 4:12) and that we have His promise that when it is proclaimed, it will effectively, infallibly accomplish His purposes (Isa. 55:11).

Evangelizing Children

Having a biblically sound understanding of repentance is no less important when sharing the gospel with children than it is when evangelizing adults, since Jesus's command to "repent and believe in the gospel" is universal. There is no "repentance lite" for children, after which they upgrade to the full version. Therefore, those who minister to children (parents, pastors, teachers) must remember that children are rebels against God (Ps. 51:5), and unless they repent, they will be under His eternal condemnation. The term *childhood innocence* may be a reality in the world of Norman Rockwell paintings, but it is heresy as far as Scripture is concerned. Everyone with children knows they are sinful creatures. The seed of jealousy has already taken root in the infant who starts screaming when his mother holds another baby in the nursery. There may or may not be an *age of accountability*, the age at which someone becomes responsible before God for his sin; regardless of this, one ought to have a sense of urgency when evangelizing young people.

But some might wonder whether it is possible for an eight-year-old to be genuinely broken over his sin. I would respond that it is not possible apart from the working of the Holy Spirit in his heart, just as it is impossible for a natural man of any age to hate and sorrow over the sin he once delighted in. Nevertheless, I do believe there are some important considerations to keep in mind that are specific to ministering to children.

First, because of their young age, their sins are relatively few and, by society's standards, minor. And with children of a compliant and cheerful disposition, it may be nearly impossible to see evidence of their internal corruption. But make no mistake; it is there and must be exposed in the light of God's law. I am not suggesting that when a child sins, a parent or teacher should scold them with moralizing statements that begin something like, "Now Johnny, the Bible says not to steal, so you shouldn't have stolen that piece of candy." Obviously, that is true, but the parent ought instead to use this opportunity to show Johnny the wickedness of his heart that led him to steal the candy. For instance, the parent might say, "Johnny, God is very generous and has given you everything you need. But you were greedy and covetous, and you weren't satisfied with God's generous provision. Do you see how evil, how full of greed and covetousness your heart is?" Of course, the age of the child will determine the vocabulary that the parent uses.

There are, however, some pitfalls that must be avoided in this type of ministry. Anger on the parent's part must be avoided at all costs. If he can't have this conversation with Johnny without getting angry, then he should save it for another time. Rather, he ought to come alongside Johnny with sympathy that comes from a right view of his own sinfulness—and even tell him about how he used to do the same sin before Jesus transformed his life and that he still must ask God for help not to do it.

Those who minister to children ought to also be careful not to oversimplify repentance and faith when explaining them to a young person. Many a well-meaning youth worker will teach a child about sin in very general terms and that the consequence for sin is hell. "How can I not go to hell?" Susie asks. The teacher replies that she needs to be sorry to God for her sins and to ask Jesus into her heart. If Susie is willing to do this (as she generally will be if she has seen pictures of Jesus hugging children, etc.), he then leads her in the "Sinner's Prayer." In this way, countless young people are inoculated against true repentance and faith. Proclaiming the gospel to children necessarily means conveying to them the realities of sin, hell, satanic bondage, divine righteousness, and justification by faith. That children should be taught about these concepts is apparent from the fact Paul discusses them in his letter to the Ephesians (2:1–18; 3:10–13; 4:22–24), which was intended to be read to children as well as adults (6:1–3).

A final tendency of which we must be wary when ministering to young people is to reduce God to only His attributes that are pleasant to think about, like His love and kindness and mercy. These are indeed precious attributes of our Maker, but they are not the only ones. Let us strive to present to children the God of Scripture, who is holy and hates sin, the Jesus who not only held babies but who also drove the money changers out of the temple and scorned the false religion of the Pharisees. Only when they understand God hates corrupt things will children be able to grasp that repentance is the work of God in the heart to make us hate sin as well.

Chapter 6

In the Path of the Holy Spirit

*Now after John was put in prison, Jesus came to Galilee, preaching the
gospel of the kingdom of God, and saying, "The time is fulfilled,
and the kingdom of God is at hand. Repent, and believe in the gospel."*
(Mark 1:14–15)

The speed and course of a river are determined by a variety of factors
such as the river's age and the topography and geology of the
surrounding land. The Brazos River in Texas, for example, is
classified as a youthful river. It has a steep gradient and is therefore
fast-moving, giving it the ability to carve out a deep channel in the
rock. The Nile River, on the other hand, is considered an old river and
flows much more slowly through its broad channel. The decisive
difference between these two rivers is clearly not in the water itself (it
has the same basic chemical makeup) but in the land through which
the water flows.

Same Spirit, Different Hearts

This is analogous to the work of the Holy Spirit in bringing a person
to repentance. As water flows through different channels in different
ways, the Holy Spirit, the living water, works repentance in the hearts
of different people in distinct ways. This is not to say that the work of
the Spirit is ultimately constrained by or dependent on the heart of

the individual as He works, for we know that "God does whatever He pleases" (Ps. 115:3). Rather, as God has seen fit to shape the hearts of people according to His purposes, His Spirit works accordingly. The flow of the water shapes the rock as much as the rock determines the course of the water.

Immediate Conviction

Sometimes the Spirit brings immediate, repentance-inducing conviction of sin into a person's heart upon hearing the gospel. One prominent example of this in Scripture is when the Jews heard the gospel on Pentecost and were "cut to the heart" and cried out, "Men and brethren, what shall we do?" (Acts 2:37). The Greek verb translated *cut* (*katanyssomai*) literally means "pierced violently" and is an intensified form of the verb used in John 19:34 to describe the spear being thrust into Jesus's side by the soldier. Simply put, the Holy Spirit drove the conviction of sin deeper into the hearts of Peter's hearers than the soldier jabbed the spear into Christ's flesh. Recognizing their fatal wound, they turned immediately to the Good Physician in repentance and faith.

Preparatory Work

In other cases, the Spirit works more gradually in the heart. One may experience a sort of spiritual awakening in which he is brought to a general awareness he is a sinner—that he has done wrong things—and even that he has violated his conscience and the law of God. Nevertheless, there is no true repentance and, therefore, no regeneration.

Legal Penitence

Often, this person will practice what theologians of previous generations called *legal repentance* (as opposed to true or evangelical repentance), which signifies a person's desire to essentially atone for sin by reforming his life and adhering strictly to God's commandments as he understands them. If the Spirit does no further work in the legal penitent's heart, he will remain a hell-bound Pharisee. The problem for these people is they have only a notional understanding of sin and do not grasp the seriousness of their condition and their own helplessness. In the modern church, we see this scenario played out in those who are constantly "rededicating" their life to Christ. They recognize their life is full of sin and that something needs to be done about it, so they roll up their sleeves and endeavor to defeat sin in their own strength. In doing so, they are like Hercules, who tried to kill the Hydra by cutting off its head, only to have two more heads grow in its place. And they remind us of the man of whom Jesus spoke in Matthew 12:43, whose soul became clean and well-ordered when the unclean spirit left him, but who wound up in a worse state when that spirit returned with "seven other spirits more wicked than himself." Multitudes die in this plight and go on to face eternal torment and misery. But for those chosen by God for salvation, legal repentance is only a marker or waypoint on their journey as the Spirit brings them to true repentance.

Examples from Scripture and Church History

The Apostle Paul

The apostle Paul (Saul) prior to his conversion was a poster child for legal penitence. According to the letter of the law, he led a blameless life (Phil. 3:6) and achieved a level of moral rectitude that few could match. But even in this, his religious fervor was not spent. So he set out to destroy the new sect called Christianity by killing its followers, who taught that righteousness came not by obedience to the law but by faith in Jesus Christ. And this he did with great zeal and efficiency.

But I suspect that after hearing the testimonies of martyrs like Stephen, his self-trust began to erode; it must have become increasingly difficult for him to maintain his religiosity. As the Spirit worked in his heart, he fought hard to hold on to his concept of legal righteousness, which had driven him for so long. For when Christ met

Saul on the road to Damascus, He said to him, "It is hard for you to kick against the goads" (Acts 9:5). Jesus acknowledged that Saul had been resisting the work of God in his heart and life, but He warned it was as futile for him to continue to fight as it is for a donkey to kick and fight when spurs are driven into its side to make it move in a certain direction.

At this point, Saul's resistance crumbled, and he repented, renouncing his righteousness, and submitted to God. His new and saving fear of God is indicated in that he was "trembling and astonished" (v. 6), and his submission is demonstrated by his question: "Lord, what do you want me to do?" Concerning this passage, Calvin writes:

> The fruit of that reprehension follows, wherewith we have said it was requisite that Paul should have been sore shaken, that his hardness might be broken. For now he offers himself as ready to do whatsoever he should command him, whom of late he despised. For when he asks what Christ would have him do, he grants him authority and power. Even the very reprobate are also terrified with the threatening of God, so that they are compelled to reverence him, and to submit themselves unto his will and pleasure; yet, nevertheless, they cease not to fret and to foster stubbornness within. But as God humbled Paul, so he wrought effectually in his heart. For it came not to pass by any goodness of nature, that Paul did more willingly submit himself to God than Pharaoh, (Exodus 7:13); but because, being like to an anvil, [Pharaoh] did, with his hardness, beat back the whips of God wherewith he was to be brought under, (even as it had been the strokes of a hammer;) but the heart of Paul was suddenly made a fleshy heart of a stony heart, after that it received softness from the Spirit of God; which softness it had not naturally.[1]

---

[1] John Calvin, *Commentary on the Book of Acts,* trans. Henry Beveridge (Grand Rapids: Christian Classics Ethereal Library, 2005), 282.

Church history is also replete with examples of men who practiced legal penitence for a time, but to whom God ultimately granted true repentance.

Augustine

As you might recall from chapter 2, Augustine spent his early years in debauchery and heresy, living with his concubine and following the teachings of the Manichaeans (a heretical sect). But while in his early twenties, he was profoundly affected by the ideas of certain Greek philosophers as well as the preaching of Ambrose, the bishop of Milan. He experienced a kind of conversion, which led him to abandon the Manichaeans and embrace Christianity. By all outward appearances he was a reformed man, yet he was still a slave to sin, as he had not been born again of the Spirit. It would be several more years before he would embrace Christ Himself through repentance and faith.

Luther

Martin Luther, though not as outwardly immoral as Augustine, also spent his youth in worldly pursuits; up to the age of twenty-one, he had little, if any, interest in Christianity. But as he was walking home one afternoon from the university where he studied law, he was caught in a thunderstorm and was nearly struck by lightning. In his distress, he cried out to Saint Anne and promised that if she would save him, he would dedicate his life to God and become a monk. He survived the storm and kept his end of the bargain. Eventually, he was ordained to the priesthood and began to teach the Bible at the University of Wittenberg.

Despite his external piety, Luther inwardly seethed with rebellion against, and hatred toward, God. He later recounted his condition in the following well-known statement: "Though I lived as a monk without reproach, I felt that I was a sinner before God with an extremely disturbed conscience. I could not believe that he was placated by my satisfaction. I did not love, yes, I hated the righteous God who punishes sinners, and secretly, if not blasphemously, certainly murmuring greatly."[2]

Luther clearly lived with a sense of his own sinfulness in the light of God's righteousness. He was convinced that his moral uprightness and works of penance (satisfaction) were insufficient to satisfy God's justice, but he had no other hope of being right with God. It was in this state Luther remained until one day, as he meditated on Romans 1:17, the Holy Spirit opened his eyes to see "the righteousness of God is that by which the righteous lives by a gift of God, namely by faith."[3] When he understood this, Luther repented, renouncing his own righteousness, and trusted in Christ alone for salvation. It is no surprise that Luther considered this passage to be his gateway to eternal life.

Bunyan

Another great Christian who went through a period of legal penitence prior to experiencing true repentance is John Bunyan. In his autobiography, *Grace Abounding to the Chief of Sinners*, Bunyan describes his young self as being "filled with all unrighteousness: the which did also so strongly work and put forth itself, both in my heart and life, and that from a child, that I had but few equals, especially considering my years, which were tender, being few, both for cursing, swearing, lying, and blaspheming the holy name of God."[4]

He continued in this wicked lifestyle until shortly after he married, at which point he read some devotional works he inherited from his father-in-law. Upon reading these books he became deeply interested in religion—so much so he began attending church twice a day. This

---

[2] Martin Luther, *Luther's Works* (St. Louis: Concordia, 1960), 34:336–37.

[3] *Luther's Works*, 337.

[4] John Bunyan, *Grace Abounding to the Chief of Sinners* (Peabody, MA: Hendrickson, 2007), 10.

awakening eventually led to the reformation of his habits; he ceased drinking, cursing, and partying, and he began to read Scripture voraciously. Bunyan became an all-around model citizen. He writes that those around him who witnessed this transformation "did take me to be a very godly man, a new and religious man, and did marvel much to see such a great and famous alteration in my life and manners."[5]

His upright conduct notwithstanding, Bunyan became more aware than ever of the corruption of his heart and began to despair of ever being right with God. Unlike Augustine and Luther, it is difficult to pinpoint the moment at which Bunyan first repented, but it must have been during this period of his life, for it often happens that the darkness of despair engulfs the true penitent's soul before God causes to shine into his heart "the light of the knowledge of the glory of God in the face of Jesus Christ" (2 Cor. 4:6). And it was not long before that light came. One day Bunyan heard a sermon on the love of Christ, and his heart was ravished by a new understanding of the mercy and grace of God embodied in the person of Christ.

If space allowed, I could go into the lives of George Whitefield and the Wesley brothers, whose times of legal penitence overlapped during their membership in the Holy Club at Oxford University, where they observed a strict set of regulations. Jonathan Edwards and David Brainerd have similar stories. But I hope the brief sketches which I have provided will suffice to illustrate that the Holy Spirit may bring people through a phase of legal penitence before granting them true repentance, just as He may also bring them to repentance immediately upon hearing the gospel for the first time.

The fact that so many great saints have experienced legal repentance leads me to believe there is benefit in it for some. It's not that a person is brought any closer to salvation or to God by it, for that would mean

---

[5] Bunyan, 17.

there is an intermediate step in the salvation process, which is certainly false. But if there is a benefit, it may be illustrated by the advantage of launching a telescope, like the Hubble, into space. We might think its main asset is that it is closer to the objects which it is viewing, but this is not the case. Considering the distance to some of the objects it has viewed (13 billion light years), being 370 miles closer is utterly inconsequential. Rather, its advantage is due to its being outside of Earth's atmosphere, which tends to distort images captured by telescopes on the ground. This interference can be likened to the effect debauched living has on the hearts of men. Therefore, God sometimes sees fit to bring them out of that lifestyle before He opens their eyes to the truth.

Before proceeding, it is important to reiterate that natural men, on whom God has bestowed no special grace and in whom the Spirit of God is doing no saving work, may experience legal repentance. It is completely within the scope of human nature, because of the influence of common grace, for a person to reform his life out of self-interest, for the sake of religion, and even in the name of Christ (right living does, after all, have its temporal benefits, and even more so if it is accompanied by the transcendent meaning religion provides). To the observer, the legal penitent may look no different than the true penitent. But when a man searches his own heart, he may learn whether the saving work of the Holy Spirit has begun.

Self-Examination

I went into some detail in the first chapter concerning the indicators of true repentance, but we might ask ourselves the following questions:

- Have I begun to hate the sin I once loved and delighted in?

- If there were no hell to pay upon death, would I still hate sin?

- Have I begun to sorrow over sin, not just because of its negative effect on my life or the lives of others but because I see I have offended God?

- Have I begun to see sin as it is—as a cancer that must be cut out?

- Is there any impulse in my heart to make war against sin and to kill it?

- Have I confessed my sin to God, not out of obligation but out of sincere distress of heart?

- Have I despaired of all hope of meriting salvation by my own righteousness and good works?

If you can answer yes to these questions, then you have good reason to believe the seed of true repentance has taken root in your heart, and you can give glory to God for this. Yet we need to be careful we do not begin to trust in these evidences but in Christ alone: "Let him who thinks he stands take heed lest he fall" (1 Cor. 10:12).

If, on the other hand, you answer most or all these questions in the negative, then you have reason to suspect your repentance may be of the legal type. If this is the case, then you have no grounds on which to hope for salvation and every reason to expect the fearsome judgment of God to descend upon you the instant you take your last breath. Upon this realization, you have several options before you:

Option 1: Decide that if you are going to hell, you might as well enjoy life in the interim and plunge yourself fully into wickedness.

Option 2: Suppress the truth and continue to trust in your own righteousness. Consulting friends and loved ones will often result in this. It's not that they want to lead you astray, but from their perspective, you appear to be an upstanding Christian. In this way, they are like the false prophets spoken of in Jeremiah 6:14, who essentially put a bandage over the people's gaping wound and spoke false and groundless words of comfort to them.

Option 3: Adopt an attitude of apathy, thinking that if God wants to grant you repentance, then He will. It is of course true that God grants repentance to whomever He wills, but He also deals with us as active agents, not passive robots.

Option 4: Seek the living God and cry out to Him for repentance and faith.

It is this fourth option I want to discuss in some detail, for it's what Christ exhorted His hearers to do when He said, "Strive to enter through the narrow gate" (Luke 13:24). Again, this is not an instruction manual concerning how to repent, as the question that one should ask is not "How do I repent?" Rather, the right question is "What are some ways in which I might avail myself to the Holy Spirit, or place myself in His path, that He may work repentance in my heart, if He chooses?" For to make repentance something one can learn to do simply by receiving man's instruction would necessarily make it a work, and we know works are no basis for salvation (Eph. 2:9; 2 Tim. 1:9, etc.).

Additionally, we must recognize God is under no obligation to grant us repentance. While it is true God grants those holy desires which have their root in Him, it is equally true that "the heart is deceitful above all things, and desperately wicked; who can know it?" (Jer. 17:9). So the man who thinks he is seeking repentance out of a pure desire to be right with God may in fact be doing so out of self-love or the desire for temporary comfort. God has made no promise to fulfill the desires of such a man. Indeed, Proverbs 10:3 tells us He "casts away the desire of the wicked." Nevertheless, beat upon the door of God's house as you would bang on the door of a police officer's house in the middle of the night if a dozen gang members were chasing you down. Keep knocking until God opens the door or you die, as the possibility of being saved is better than certainty of eternal torment.

But how does one avail himself to or put himself in the way of the Holy Spirit? Here are some means that have proven helpful for me and others. You may use these or any other legitimate means, but do not trust for a moment in any means or in your use of them. Instead, put all your confidence in God, who is a "rewarder of those who diligently seek Him" (Heb. 11:6). Remember that *He* must grant you repentance (2 Tim. 2:25), and plead with Him to do so. Ask Him to work in your heart and mind and to make effective the means you employ.

First, strive to be convinced of your own wickedness. Jesus is a physician not to the healthy but to the sick. Therefore, make every effort to see your spiritual sickness, the plague of sin that is in your heart. The Jews of the prophet Jeremiah's day were steeped in idolatry, making offerings to idols in the Valley of Hinnom. Perhaps initially they felt some guilt and remorse about it, but they had suppressed those feelings and justified their wicked behavior for so long they no longer recognized it as sin. God, speaking to them through Jeremiah, said to them, "How can you say, 'I am not polluted, I have not gone after the Baals'? See your way in the valley; know what you have done" (Jer. 2:23). This same advice I give to you: know what you have done. Stop suppressing your guilt and justifying your sin by calling it "normal" or by comparing yourself to others. Every person will be judged by God by His righteous and unchanging standard, the Ten Commandments, not by the sliding scale of public opinion.

Linger long in meditating on God's law, not just on the words of the law but on the spirit and intent of each command. Think about all the times you have committed murder by harboring hatred or contempt toward someone in your heart (Matt. 5:21–22). Consider the many adulterous affairs you have engaged in through your lust (Matt. 5:28). Ponder the jealousy of God for your affection and how you have spurned Him by worshiping idols—giving your heart to other people and objects. Meditate also on the first three chapters of Romans, in which Paul demonstrates how all unbelievers stand guilty before the righteous God and justly fall under His fierce anger. Reflect frequently on specific sins you have committed, both what you have done and what you have left undone. Confess these sins in detail to God, and petition Him to turn your heart against them.

Second, do not indulge your sinful appetites, for every occasion on which you do serves only to dull your conscience and decrease the probability that you will come under the saving convictions of the Holy Spirit. We should not confuse the convictions of conscience with those of the Spirit; they are not the same thing. Nevertheless, a sensitive conscience is a powerful tool in the hand of the Spirit. While it is true that you cannot cure yourself, as long as you continue to drink the carcinogen of sin, you should not expect to be healed from your spiritual cancer. Further, if you wait passively for God to turn your heart against sin before you attempt to turn from your wickedness, you will be like the fool described in a poem, who, before he would cross the river, "stood all day at the riverside till all the water should run by."[6]

Declare war against sin. In so doing, you will become painfully aware of the power of sin in your heart and of your own pathetic inability to defeat it. If you consider yourself strong enough that you could overcome your sin if you tried, you are like the little poodle who barks at the Doberman and pulls on the leash, eager to show his strength. Of course, if the leash ever broke, he would quickly realize he was mistaken. Engage sin in battle, and you will be humbled, if nothing else.

---

[6] Henry Scougal, *The Life of God in the Soul of Man* (n.p.: Rough Draft Publishing, 2012), 73.

Do not make light of any sin, even those which seem to be universal in the culture. Treat all sin with the severity it deserves. Gluttony destroys the soul as much as murder, and filling the mind with debased things from the television, computer, or smartphone is as deadly as doing the things depicted.

Third, think often of your death, the righteous judgment of God, and the wrath that will be poured out on the impenitent. We are told in Scripture that "it is appointed for men to die once, but after this the judgment" (Heb. 9:27). Christ came into the world the first time to save men, but when He returns it will be unto judgment. Christ came the first time as a lamb to be slaughtered, but He will return to slaughter His enemies (2 Thess. 1:8). Bear in mind that some of these enemies will appeal for mercy by calling Him "Lord" but will receive none. When you appear before His judgment throne, not only will you be held accountable for every action but also for every word that has come from your mouth (Matt. 12:36) and every thought that has gone through your mind (Heb. 4:12). Your life and your heart will be completely exposed, and His judgment will be thorough. Those thoughts you've had, which you would have been embarrassed to tell your most intimate friend, will be on display for all to see. And when the proceedings are complete, and you are cast into eternal torment, all your loved ones who have been watching will applaud the perfect justice of God (Ps. 91:8; Isa. 66:24; Rev. 20:12). There will not be a single advocate who tries to plead your case before the Judge.

What will this eternal torment be like? Do not listen to those who describe it as total separation from God. It is the separation from God's love and mercy and friendship. But the full force of His wrath will certainly be present in hell for all eternity. Scripture describes it as "outer darkness" (Matt. 8:12), where there will be "weeping and gnashing of teeth" (Luke 13:28), and the place where "[the] worm does not die and the fire is not quenched" (Mark 9:44). The suffering that will be experienced there will far exceed the soul's capacity to bear up under it, and the soul will be eternally sinking into greater and greater despair. Listen to one preacher's treatment of this topic:

> We can conceive but little of the matter; we cannot conceive what that sinking of the soul in such a case is. But to help your conception, imagine yourself to be cast into a fiery oven, or of a great furnace, where your pain would be as much greater than that occasioned by accidentally touching a coal of fire as the heat is greater. Imagine also that your body were to lie in there for a quarter of an hour, all the while full of quick sense; what horror would you feel at the entrance of such a furnace! And how long would that quarter of an hour seem to you! And after you had endured it for one minute, how overbearing would it be to you to think that you had to endure the other fourteen! But what would be the effect on your soul, if you knew that you must lie there enduring that torment for a full twenty-four hours! And how much greater would be the effect, if you knew you must endure it for a whole year, and how vastly greater still, if you knew you must endure it for a thousand years! O then, how would your heart sink, if you thought, if you knew, that you must bear it forever and ever! That there would be no end! That after millions and millions of ages, your torment would be no nearer to an end, than ever it was: and that you never, never should be delivered![7]

Do not avoid thinking about this topic because it is painful; to experience the reality of eternal torment will be far worse than merely thinking about it. Think much of hell, and let it increase your resolve to obtain true repentance.

Fourth, read frequently and think deeply about the sufferings of Christ. Ponder the physical agony of the beatings that He endured and of the intense pain of being nailed to that Roman tool of torture, the cross. Consider the mental anguish that this Lover of souls

---

[7] William C. Nichols, ed., *Seeking God: Jonathan Edwards' Evangelism Contrasted with Modern Methodologies* (Ames, Iowa: International Outreach, 2001), 134–35.

suffered as cruel men mocked Him and all His closest friends deserted Him. But most importantly, meditate on how Christ was given as a substitutionary sacrifice. As such, not only was His body slaughtered but He also bore the sins of the world and the Father's fierce and consuming wrath toward sinners.

Jesus was certainly not the weak coward some make Him out to be, trembling in fear of the physical pain He would encounter. Rather, when He sweat drops of blood and begged the Father to let the cup pass from Him, it was at the prospect of drinking from the cup of God's wrath and being utterly forsaken by His Father, who is too pure to look upon sin. Many love the famous words of John 3:16, and rightly so. But few take notice of the statement a few verses later which says, "He who believes in the Son has everlasting life; whoever does not believe in the Son shall not see life, but the wrath of God abides on him" (v. 36). So for those who repent and believe, God's holy hatred (Ps. 5:5) is lifted from them and placed on Christ on the cross, and they enter into God's perfect love. But those who remain impenitent and faithless are a breath away from being under that hatred for all of eternity.

Consider also the purpose of Christ's unimaginable sufferings. In them He purchased nothing less for the elect than the riches of God's glorious grace, by which, through faith, they enter into union with Him, receiving His perfect righteousness and the boundless riches of the inheritance the Father has promised the Son. Meditate on Romans 8:32 until you can bear no longer to be on the outside: "He who did not spare His own Son, but delivered Him up for us all, how shall He not with Him also freely give us all things?"

Finally, if you sense the Holy Spirit is beginning to bring you under convictions for sin, welcome and embrace them with all your heart. Do not hinder the Spirit's work by trying to eliminate them, no matter how painful they are. Give the Spirit free access to the darkest recesses of your soul, that He might expose to you the depths of your depravity and cause you to feel the full weight of the burden of sin. Seek no other relief from this burden than the shed blood of Christ, which is the only means which God has appointed for the comfort and healing of the brokenhearted.

When comfort floods into your soul, Christ will become so sweet and precious to you that all the mental anguish you previously experienced will be swallowed up in joy. Thus will you enter into the kingdom of God. "The time [has come] and the kingdom of God is at hand. Repent, and believe in the gospel" (Mark 1:15).

Appendix 1: My Repentance Journey

The early part of my spiritual journey was in many ways typical of American middle-class "churched" youth. From the age of about seven, I attended a non-denominational, evangelical church. I remember hearing the invitation to accept Jesus into my heart, and I really wanted to—and tried for the next few years—but it never seemed to "work." My heart remained unchanged; I continued to live in rebellion against God and every authority figure He placed in my life. For the most part, I lived without passion or purpose. But one thing I did love was basketball. Like most of my friends, I dreamed of becoming a professional basketball player. But that aspiration took a big hit when I failed to make the team as a freshman. I remember feeling devastated for about a week. I couldn't understand why God would let that happen when He knew how desperately I wanted to play and how much glory I could get for Him if I ever achieved this dream.

It was somewhere around this time when my father gave me a book written by a Christian basketball player. I read it several times through and began to yearn for the purpose, happiness, and success that characterized his life. It seemed to me that God "worked" for him, and if God was good enough for him, then He would be good enough for me. It's not that I was a total pragmatist; I had always believed in God, so there was some basis for my new desire apart from wanting God to do for me what He had done for that man. But reading his story caused me to want God to be a major part of my life.

A few weeks after reading this book, I raised my hand at church when the pastor gave the invitation. Ironically, he didn't see me, but I nevertheless considered that to be the day Jesus came into my heart. From this point, my general outlook and attitude began to change. Things started to go well for me, and I had a level of happiness I had never known before. My new passion and focus made me a better basketball player, and I made the team the following year. Many of my negative behaviors seemed to melt away, and I was confident I had finally become a Christian.

But over the next decade, the passion wore off, and many aspects of the old self returned. I found myself constantly battling unbelief. I was drowning in unbelief and idolatry, all the while trying to convince myself I really believed in God and loved Him with all my heart. This inner dissonance, combined with the stress I felt as a teacher in inner-city Brooklyn, brought me to the verge of a nervous breakdown.

Then one Sunday I was sitting next to a friend of mine in church (who knew nothing of my struggle), and he handed me a slip of paper he had torn off his bulletin on which were written the words of Proverbs 3:5–6: "Trust in the LORD with all your heart, and lean not on your own understanding; in all your ways acknowledge Him, and He will direct your path." My friend turned to me and whispered, "God wants me to give this to you."

The instant the words of this verse entered my mind, it was like a light turned on in my soul, and God made the reality of Himself obvious to me. Up until that moment, I had constantly vacillated between fundamentalist Christianity, New Age Gnosticism, and skepticism. But then and there God made Himself and His Word appear absolutely trustworthy before the eyes of my mind; I instantly abandoned my unbelief, and from that point on began to pray with the conviction that God is real and to read my Bible with confidence in its veracity. Not surprisingly, I experienced marked spiritual growth over the year following that event—probably more than the previous ten years combined.

By God's grace, this growth continued, to greater or lesser degrees, over the next several years. I learned what it means to seek the Lord through meditation on Scripture and through prayer. I came to understand, believe in, and love God's sovereignty, which fostered in me deeper and more durable faith. And God gradually exposed corruption in my heart I had not even been aware of. That the Lord was powerfully at work during this period of my life is undeniable. Nevertheless, I was soon to discover a crack in my spiritual foundation, the repair of which would require God to demolish the entire house.

Repentance was a term I was familiar with but did not fully understand—nor did I want to, I might add. It seemed to me that the path that I was on was working, so I simply heeded the old adage, "If it ain't broke, don't fix it." At least nothing appeared to me to be broken. Sure, I struggled with the same sins time and again, but *who doesn't?* I reasoned. But when I read what some of the saints of old— Jonathan Edwards, John Owen, and George Whitefield, to name a few—had to say about repentance and true conversion, my soul was disturbed, and my security, shaken. Their views were foreign to me, almost unintelligible; it was like finding directions written two hundred years ago, in which the author referred to landmarks that no longer exist. But I understood enough to know that if their conception of repentance was scriptural, then I was missing something.

I remember one instance when, after reading Edwards's *Religious Affections*, I went to my knees and asked God to show me whether I had truly repented of my sins, whether I was actually walking with Him. I didn't hear anything from God right away, and not wanting to be in limbo regarding my eternal state, I comforted myself with the fact that I had said "the prayer" and my life seemed to show evidence of genuine conversion—consistency in the spiritual disciplines (prayer, meditation, fasting, etc.), lack of egregious outward sins, and a fruitful ministry in the church. And so I spoke peace to myself like the false prophets of ancient Israel (Ezekiel 13:10). Nevertheless, my soul was becoming increasingly unsettled by the possibility I had never really repented.

Then one morning I downloaded a sermon called "Ten Shekels and a Shirt," preached by Paris Reidhead in the mid-1960s, in which he rails against the pragmatic, humanistic spirit which characterizes the modern church. As I listened to the message, God, I believe, answered my prayer through the following passage:

> What about you? Why did you repent? I'd like to see ... people repent on Biblical terms again. George Whitefield knew it. He stood on Boston Commons speaking to twenty thousand people and he said, "Listen sinners, you're monsters, monsters of iniquity! You deserve Hell! And the worst of your crimes is in that criminals though you've been, you haven't had the good grace to see it!" He said, "If you will not weep for your sins and your crimes against a Holy God, George Whitefield will weep for you!" That man would put his head back and he would sob like a baby. Why? Because they were in danger of Hell? No! But because they were monsters of iniquity, who didn't even see their sin or care about their crimes. You see the difference? ... The difference is, here's somebody trembling because he is going to be hurt in Hell. And he has no sense of the enormity of his guilt! And no sense of the enormity of his crime! And no sense of his insult against Deity! He's only trembling because his skin is about to be singed. He's afraid, and I submit to you that whereas fear is good office work in preparing us for grace, it's no place to stop. And the Holy Ghost doesn't stop there. That's the reason why people cannot savingly receive Christ until they've repented. And persons cannot repent who have not been convicted. And conviction is the work of the Holy Ghost that helps a sinner to see that he is a criminal before God and deserves all God's wrath. And if God were to send him to the lowest corner of ... Hell (for) ten

eternities, that he deserved it all—and a hundred-fold more.
...He's seen his crimes![1]

Right away I realized I had never repented in the way Reidhead was describing. Now if he had been the first person to call into question my conception and experience of repentance, I probably would have brushed him off as an overzealous hellfire preacher. But he was not the first, nor would he be the last. Even after I heard that message, God continued to confirm its validity through other messages and books as well as Scriptures I happened to be studying at the time.

It became crystal clear to me I had never repented, and therefore, my soul was in a desperate plight. This was a startling—no, terrifying—realization. But worse still, I saw that my heart was hard and I had a callous attitude toward sin, which were the products of both my sinful nature and the many times I had spoken peace to myself when my condition was exposed. I knew I needed to repent; I understood intellectually I was a sinner but had no real sense of the gravity of my sin or, in Reidhead's words, the enormity of my guilt. I was therefore unable to repent and, thus, rendered utterly helpless. The following excerpt from my journal illustrates the despair I felt:

> My heart is leprous. I feel no hatred for my sin but only give mental assent to the fact that I am a sinner and that I am offensive to the Maker of the heavens, who is holy. And that which I have mistaken for repentance is only the intellectual knowledge that what I am doing is not right, combined with the fear of punishment. What makes it all the more deplorable is that I feared only temporal punishment and not the eternal fury of God's wrath in Hell, which will certainly be the punishment

---

[1] "Ten Shekels and a Shirt," Paris Reidhead Bible Teaching Ministries, accessed December 29, 2017, http://www.parisreidheadbibleteaching ministries. org/Ten_Shekels_and_A_Shirt.html.

pronounced on me when I stand before the Judge of all the earth, unless He is pleased to open my eyes before that day, while there is still time to repent.

At that point, I was at a loss as to how to proceed. I knew nothing I did would obligate God to change my heart and grant me repentance, but it also occurred to me it was by God's mercy He had made me aware of my plight.

I think it's worth digressing for a moment to note that if this had happened to me at an earlier point in my life, I would have almost certainly forsaken God and the hope of salvation altogether. My reasoning would have gone something like this: "If I am going to fall under the judgment of God anyway, then I might as well live like the son of hell that I am and have fun while I can." But thanks be to God that in the years prior, He was imparting to my mind a grander and more compelling and desirable view of Himself, along with a longing for eternal things. So when He revealed to me I was not in good standing with Him, I wanted more than ever to turn to Him rather than away from Him. Knowing He alone could grant me repentance (1 Tim. 2:25), I began to plead with the Lord to open my eyes to see His perfect righteousness and holiness as well as my own depravity. I meditated on the Ten Commandments, reflecting on the aspects of God's nature and character that are revealed in each one (e.g., His exclusivity, jealousy, kindness, and compassion) and specific ways I had violated His commands. Here is a pertinent passage from my journal:

> Still impenitent, hard-hearted, insensible of my own vileness. I've been meditating on the law of God for two weeks, hoping that I might be broken as I see God's holy nature and righteous requirements, and myself in light of these, but to no avail. I have seen with certainty that I am an idolater, God-hater, blasphemer, Sabbath-breaker, liar, adulterer, coveter and murderer. Nevertheless, this knowledge has not brought me to repentance because it has not pierced my heart, but has only been brought

before my mind. So I remain in my sin, without Christ and devoid of hope.

The way in which I characterized myself in this entry might seem like over-the-top self-condemnation. But it was the most accurate self-assessment I had ever conducted. I understood for the first time what Jesus meant when He said if a man has hatred and contempt for another in his heart, he has committed murder, and if he looks at a woman with lust, he has committed adultery. He was telling the Pharisees (and by implication, you and me) it is possible to obey the letter of the law—to keep oneself from committing the act of murder, for example—but to be a murderer nonetheless by transgressing against the spirit of the law. I understood this principle also applies to the other commandments, which meant I was in violation of all of them.

Many of those closest to me, in whom I confided what I was going through, thought I was being unnecessarily hard on myself. They assumed I had simply been overly affected by a passionate sermon and that it would soon wear off. But my wife, Laura, knowing I am not easily moved, was the first to acknowledge that my distress was genuine and with good cause. She expressed the sentiment I suspect may have been in the minds of others, making them quick to dismiss my concerns: if it is really true that John isn't right with God, then I need to consider *my own* spiritual status.

It was clear to me God was at work in my heart, but I didn't perceive any significant changes in my heart over the next month. Then one morning, I was reading Romans 3, in which Paul, referring to impenitent sinners, writes:

As it is written:

"There is none righteous, no, not one;
There is none who understands;
There is none who seeks after God.

They have all turned aside;
They have together become unprofitable;
There is none who does good, no, not one."
"Their throat is an open tomb;
With their tongues they have practiced deceit";
"The poison of asps is under their lips";
"Whose mouth is full of cursing and bitterness."
"Their feet are swift to shed blood;
Destruction and misery are in their ways;
And the way of peace they have not known."
"There is no fear of God before their eyes."

Now we know that whatever the law says, it says to those who are under the law, that every mouth may be stopped, and all the world may become guilty before God. Therefore by the deeds of the law no flesh will be justified in His sight, for by the law is the knowledge of sin. (Rom. 3:10–20)

As I read these verses, I sensed for the first time in my life the severity of my sin. I felt the reality of my throat being an open tomb. I hated that my idolatry had kept me from truly seeking God. I was broken over the bitterness and cursing emanating from my corrupt heart. And I knew I stood condemned under the righteous law of God—and that I fully deserved God's condemnation and wrath. I owned my sin and was at last brought to repentance as God caused His word, by the power of the Holy Spirit, to penetrate my stony heart.

Still, I wasn't sure if my repentance was sufficient. I also didn't know what the next step should be. God did, though. On the way to work, I happened to notice a sermon on my iPod titled "Don't Expect Perfect Repentance" by Paul Washer. In it, he argues that one shouldn't expect his initial repentance to be at the same depth and intensity as that of someone who has been walking with God for forty years. What matters is that the seed of true repentance has been planted. And I knew that seed had indeed been planted in my heart.

During my break that afternoon, I read a sermon preached by George Whitefield in the eighteenth century titled "The Means of Grace." It was probably the fifth time I had read it that month, but this time tears of joy filled my eyes as I read Whitefield's words:

> If any of you are willing to be reconciled to God, God the Father, Son, and Holy Ghost, is willing to be reconciled to you. O then, though you have no peace as yet, come away to Jesus Christ; he is our peace, he is our peace-maker—he has made peace betwixt God and offending man. Would you have peace with God? Away, then, to God through Jesus Christ, who has purchased peace.[2]

I found myself whispering, "Yes! Yes! God wants to reconcile me, a depraved sinner, to Himself through Jesus Christ; I am willing!" Christ became indescribably precious to me in that moment, and all I could do was fall to my knees and worship Him.

That evening I learned that God had moved Laura to spend the day pleading with Him on my behalf, which left me barely able to contain the joy and gratitude I felt toward this infinitely gracious God.

The following morning, I began reading where I had left off in Romans 3: "But now the righteousness of God apart from the law is revealed, being witnessed by the Law and the Prophets, even the righteousness of God, through faith in Jesus Christ, to all and on all who believe. For there is no difference" (Rom. 3:21–22).

The word *gospel* is translated from the Greek word *evangelion*, meaning "good message" or "good news." I had learned this years ago. And I could have told you that the good news of Christianity is that Christ came to earth, lived a perfect life, and died for our sins, and to be "saved," one simply needs to believe in Him. But after having seen my guilt under the law and the consequent wrath and condemnation

---

[2] George Whitefield, "The Method of Grace," in *Christian Classics Ethereal Library*, accessed January 6, 2018, www.ccel.org/ccel/whitefield/ sermons.lx.html.

I deserved for violating an infinitely holy and righteous God, the reality of God imputing His righteousness to me through my faith became truly good news.

When I tell my story to other Christians, the first question they generally ask is "So you think your entire experience with Christianity before repentance was a lie?" During the time when I was desperately seeking repentance, I would have answered that question in the affirmative. But having come to the other side of it, my response is that I don't think it was all self-deception, though there was plenty of that.

The biographies of famous saints like John Bunyan, Oswald Chambers, and Hudson Taylor do not always make it clear at which point they were born again. They go through several "conversion" experiences before they enter into the fullness of the Christian life. It is important to distinguish between justification, the point at which one is cleansed of his sins and becomes the righteousness of Christ, and sanctification, which is the lifelong process of being conformed to Christ's image. Nevertheless, the distinction is not always crystal clear in a person's life.

I think Zechariah 4:10 is relevant to my experience. The context of that passage is that the Jewish exiles, led by a man named Zerubbabel, have returned to Jerusalem and are beginning to rebuild the temple. At this point, they have only laid the foundation, which seems to them like a small thing. But God says to the prophet Zechariah, "Who has despised the day of small things?" In other words, though it is not completed, and though it appears insignificant, it is part of the process God has ordained to accomplish His work, the rebuilding of the temple.

I do not want to despise the day of small things in my own life, even in hindsight. I believe the Holy Spirit was working in me since I first professed faith in Christ as a teenager. He awakened me to an interest in spiritual things and to some level of concern for my soul. He subsequently preserved me and kept me from pursuing a course of life that would have ultimately been destructive. Then God enabled me to trust His word, which is a prerequisite for knowing Him, as He reveals Himself through it. All those things were, I believe, the clearing of the land and the laying of the foundation for the work of repentance and faith He would later do in me.

In the years since my conversion, God has graciously granted me greater depth of repentance, along with more love for Jesus Christ. My heart soars when I think about the reality that I have no righteousness of my own and Christ is all my righteousness (1 Cor. 1:30).

Appendix 2: Hymns to Cultivate Repentance

I have noticed a tendency in some the churches I've attended to sing almost exclusively songs that are upbeat and intended to evoke positive emotions. And I think there is solid scriptural support for the singing of joyful songs when God's people assemble. However, I also believe there is a place in corporate worship for songs that evoke what most people would classify as negative emotions, such as sorrow and heaviness. This is supported by James 4:9, where he tells Christians to afflict themselves and to exchange their laughter for sorrow. Some believers are at a place in their spiritual walk where they need to do this—probably more than we realize.

If we truly believe, as Luther said, that repentance is a lifelong endeavor, then we should be doing things to cultivate it when we gather. One way to do this is to sing songs that are conducive to repentance. I am not suggesting we try to get people into a certain emotional state, but we should use the gift which God has given us to accomplish His ends. It is indisputable music has a profound effect on the emotions, and it is therefore a tool that the Holy Spirit may use to stir up godly sorrow. Colossians 3:16 instructs us to teach and admonish one another with psalms, hymns, and spiritual songs. This is exactly what repentance hymns help us do: theologically rich lyrics help build in our hearts and minds a vocabulary of repentance, while the music shapes our emotions and teaches us what repentance *feels* like. Worship professor Scott Aniol has suggested that music sounds like emotions feel and can therefore communicate directly to the heart. He argues that if we want deep, sincere repentance for ourselves and our fellow believers, we need to be intentional about the songs we choose for corporate (and personal) worship.[1]

The following nine hymns dealing with repentance can be found on Scott's website (Religious Affections Ministries) as well as in the hymnal he has recently produced.[2]

---

[1] Scott Aniol, *Sound Worship* (n.p.: Religious Affections Ministries, 2010), 67–70.
[2] http://religiousaffections.org/hymns, accessed June 19, 2018.

Depth of Mercy! Can There Be?
CANTERBURY

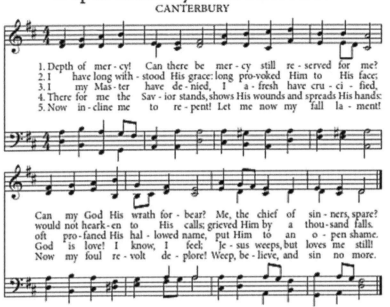

1. Depth of mer-cy! Can there be mer-cy still re-served for me?
2. I have long with-stood His grace: long pro-voked Him to His face;
3. I my Mas-ter have de-nied, I a-fresh have cru-ci-fied,
4. There for me the Sav-ior stands, shows His wounds and spreads His hands:
5. Now in-cline me to re-pent! Let me now my fall la-ment!

Can my God His wrath for-bear? Me, the chief of sin-ners, spare?
would not heark-en to His calls; grieved Him by a thou-sand falls.
oft pro-faned His hal-lowed name, put Him to an o-pen shame.
God is love! I know, I feel; Je-sus weeps, but loves me still!
Now my foul re-volt de-plore! Weep, be-lieve, and sin no more.

WORDS: Charles Wesley, 1740
MUSIC: Orlando Gibbons, 1623

7.7.7.7

A Debtor to Mercy Alone
TREWEN

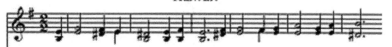

1. A debt - or to mer - cy a - lone, of cov - e-nant mer - cy I sing;
2. The work which His good-ness be - gan, the arm of His strength will com-plete;
3. My name from the palms of His hands e - ter - ni-ty will not e - rase;

nor fear, with Your right-eous-ness on, my per-son and of-f'ring to bring.
His prom - ise is yea and a - men, and nev - er was for - feit-ed yet.
im - pressed on His heart it re-mains, in marks of in - del - i-ble grace.

The ter - rors of law and of God with me can have noth - ing to do;
Things fu-ture, nor things that are now, nor all things be - low or a - bove,
Yes, I to the end shall en - dure, as sure as the ear - nest is giv'n;

my Sav-ior's o - be-dience and blood hide all my trans-gres-sions from view.
can make Him His pur-pose for - go, or sev - er my soul from His love.
more hap - py, but not more se - cure, the glo - ri-fied spir - its in heav'n.

WORDS: Augustus M. Toplady, 1771, alt.
MUSIC: David Emlyn Evans, 1895

LMD

Psalm 51

God, Be Merciful to Me

REDHEAD

1. God, be mer-ci-ful to me, on Thy grace I rest my plea;
2. My trans-gres-sions I con-fess, grief and guilt my soul op-press;
3. I am e-vil, born in sin; Thou de-sir-est truth with-in.
4. Bro-ken, hum-bled to the dust by Thy wrath and judg-ment just,
5. Gra-cious God, my heart re-new, make my spir-it right and true;
6. Sin-ners then shall learn from me and re-turn, O God, to Thee;

plen-teous in com-pas-sion Thou, blot out my trans-gres-sions now;
I have sinned a-gainst Thy grace and pro-voked Thee to Thy face;
Thou a-lone my Sav-ior art, teach Thy wis-dom to my heart;
let my con-trite heart re-joice and in glad-ness hear Thy voice;
cast me not a-way from Thee, let Thy Spir-it dwell in me;
Sav-ior, all my guilt re-move, and my tongue shall sing Thy love;

wash me, make me pure with-in, cleanse, O cleanse me from my sin.
I con-fess Thy judg-ment just, speech-less, I Thy mer-cy trust.
make me pure, Thy grace be-stow, wash me whit-er than the snow.
from my sins O hide Thy face, blot them out in bound-less grace.
Thy sal-va-tion's joy im-part, stead-fast make my will-ing heart.
touch my si-lent lips, O Lord, and my mouth shall praise ac-cord.

7. Not the formal sacrifice
   hath acceptance in Thy eyes;
   broken hearts are in Thy sight
   more than sacrificial rite;
   contrite spirit, pleading cries,
   Thou, O God, wilt not despise.

8. Prosper Zion in Thy grace
   and her broken walls replace;
   then our righteous sacrifice
   shall delight Thy holy eyes;
   free-will offerings, gladly made,
   on Thy altar shall be laid.

WORDS: **Psalm 51**; *The Psalter*, 1912
MUSIC: Richard Redhead, 1853

7.7.7.7.7.7

Psalm 32

How Blest Is He Whose Trespass
WIE LIEBLICH IST DER MAIEN

1. How blest is he whose tres - pass hath free - ly been for - giv'n,
2. While I kept guilt - y si - lence my strength was spent with grief;
3. So let the god - ly seek Thee in times when Thou art near;

whose sin is whol - ly cov - ered be - fore the sight of heav'n,
Thy hand was heav - y on me, my soul found no re - lief;
no whelm-ing floods shall reach them nor cause their hearts to fear.

to whom the LORD in mer - cy im - put-eth not his sin,
but when I owned my tres - pass, my sin hid not from Thee;
In Thee, O LORD, I hide me; Thou sav-est me from ill,

who hath a guile - less spir - it, whose heart is true with - in.
when I con-fessed trans-gres - sion, then Thou for - gav - est me.
and songs of Thy sal - va - tion my heart with rap-ture thrill.

WORDS: Psalm 32; *The Psalter*, 1912
MUSIC: Johann Steurlein, 1575

7.6.7.6.D

How Sad Our State
SASHA

1. How sad our state by na-ture is, our sin, how deep it stains;
2. My soul o-beys th' al-might-y call, and runs to this re - lief;
3. Stretch out Thine arm, vic - tor-ious King, my reign - ing sins sub - due;

and Sa - tan binds our cap-tive minds fast in his slav-ish chains.
I would be-lieve Thy prom-ise, Lord, O help my un-be - lief.
and drive the drag-on from his seat, with all his hell-ish crew.

But there's a voice of sov-'reign grace sounds from the sa - cred Word,
Un - to the foun-tain of Thy blood, In - car - nate God, I fly;
A guilt - y, weak, and help-less worm, on Thy kind arms I fall;

"Ho, ye de-spair-ing sin-ners, come, and trust up-on the Lord."
here let me wash my spot-ted soul, from crimes of deep-est dye.
be Thou my strength and right-cous-ness, my Je - sus and my all.

WORDS: Isaac Watts, 1707
MUSIC: Joan J. Pinkston, 1998

CMD

SASHA © 1998 Joan J. Pinkston. Used by permission.

127

Lord, I Deserve Thy Deepest Wrath

KEDRON

1. Lord, I de-serve Thy deep-est wrath, un-grate-ful, faith-less I have been; no ter-rors have my soul de-terred, nor good-ness wooed me from my sin.
2. My heart is vile, my mind de-praved, my flesh re-bels a-gainst Thy will; I am pol-lut-ed in Thy sight, yet, Lord have mer-cy on me still!
3. With-out de-fense to Thee I look, to Thee the on-ly Sav-ior fly; with-out a hope, with-out a friend, in deep dis-tress to Thee I cry.
4. Speak peace to me, my sins for-give, dwell Thou with-in my heart, O God; the guilt and pow'r of sin re-move, and fit me for Thy blest a-bode.

WORDS: Basil Manly, *The Baptist Psalmody*, 1850
MUSIC: attr. Elkanah Kelsay Dare, 1799

LM

No, Not Despairingly
NENTHORN

1. No, not des - pair - ing - ly come I to Thee; no, not dis -
2. Ah! Mine in - i - qui - ty crim - son has been, in - fi - nite,
3. Lord, I con - fess to Thee sad - ly my sin; all I am,
4. Faith - ful and just art Thou, for - giv - ing all; lov - ing and
5. Then all is peace and light this soul with - in; thus shall I

trust - ing - ly bend I the knee; sin hath gone o - ver me,
in - fi - nite, sin up - on sin; sin of not lov - ing Thee,
tell to Thee, all I have been; purge Thou my sin a - way,
kind art Thou when poor ones call; Lord, let the cleans - ing blood,
walk with Thee, the loved Un - seen; lean - ing on Thee, my God,

yet is this still my plea, Je - sus hath died.
sin of not trust - ing Thee, in - fi - nite sin.
wash Thou my soul this day; Lord, make me clean.
blood of the Lamb of God, pass o'er my soul.
guid - ed a - long the road, noth - ing be - tween.

WORDS: Horatius Bonar, 1866   6.4.6.4.6.6.4
MUSIC: Thomas Legerwood Hately, 19th cent.

Psalm 130

Out of the Depths I Cry to Thee

AUS TIEFER NOT

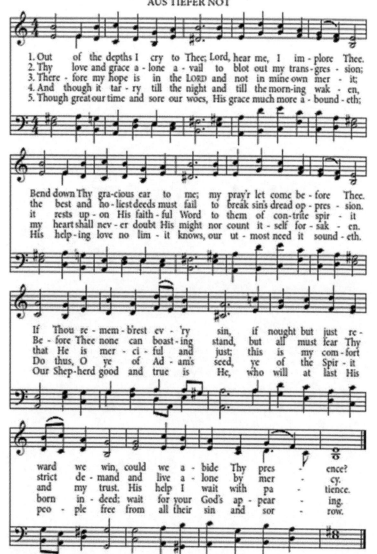

1. Out of the depths I cry to Thee; Lord, hear me, I im-plore Thee.
2. Thy love and grace a-lone a-vail to blot out my trans-gres-sion;
3. There-fore my hope is in the LORD and not in mine own mer-it;
4. And though it tar-ry till the night and till the morn-ing wak-en,
5. Though great our time and sore our woes, His grace much more a-bound-eth;

Bend down Thy gra-cious ear to me; my pray'r let come be-fore Thee.
the best and ho-liest deeds must fail to break sin's dread op-pres-sion.
it rests up-on His faith-ful Word to them of con-trite spir-it
my heart shall nev-er doubt His might nor count it-self for-sak-en.
His help-ing love no lim-it knows, our ut-most need it sound-eth.

If Thou re-mem-b'rest ev-'ry sin, if nought but just re-
Be-fore Thee none can boast-ing stand, but all must fear Thy
that He is mer-ci-ful and just; this is my com-fort
Do thus, O ye of Ad-am's seed, ye of the Spir-it
Our Shep-herd good and true is He, who will at last His

ward we win, could we a-bide Thy pres-ence?
strict de-mand and live a-lone by mer-cy.
and my trust. His help I wait with pa-tience.
born in-deed; wait for your God's ap-pear-ing.
peo-ple free from all their sin and sor-row.

WORDS: Psalm 130; Martin Luther, 1524; tr. Catherine Winkworth, 1863, alt.   8.7.8.7.8.8.7
MUSIC: Martin Luther, 1524

Rock of Ages, Cleft for Me
REDHEAD

1. Rock of Ag - es, cleft for me, let me hide my - self in Thee;
2. Not the la - bors of my hands can ful - fil Thy Law's de-mands;
3. Noth - ing in my hand I bring, sim - ply to Thy cross I cling.
4. While I draw this fleet-ing breath, when mine eye - lids close in death,

let the wa - ter and the blood from Thy wound - ed side which flowed,
could my zeal no res - pite know, could my tears for - ev - er flow,
Na - ked, come to Thee for dress; help-less, look to Thee for grace;
when I soar to worlds un-known, see Thee on Thy judg-ment throne,

be of sin the dou - ble cure; cleanse me from its guilt and pow'r.
all for sin could not a - tone; Thou must save, and Thou a - lone.
foul, I to the foun - tain fly; wash me, Sav-ior, or I die!
Rock of Ag - es, cleft for me, let me hide my - self in Thee.

WORDS: Augustus M. Toplady, 1776
MUSIC: Richard Redhead, 1853
7.7.7.7.7.7

131

Works Cited

"Hope for Healing." Luis Palau Association. Accessed June 19, 2018. http://legacy.palau.org/resources/articles/spiritualgrowth/item/hope-for-healing.

"Whatever Happened to the Clear Invitation?" Christianity Today. Accessed January 2, 2018. http://www.christianitytoday.com/pastors/1995/spring/5l2052.html.

Aniol, Scott. *Sound Worship.* N.p.: Religious Affections Ministries, 2010.

Augustine. *Confessions.* Translated by Albert C. Outler. New York: Barnes and Noble, 1997.

Bright, Bill. "Have You Heard of the Four Spiritual Laws?" Would You Like to Know God Personally? Accessed December 9, 2018. http://www.4laws.com/laws/englishkgp/default.htm.

Bunyan, John. *Grace Abounding to the Chief of Sinners.* Peabody, MA: Hendrickson, 2007.

———. *The Pilgrim's Progress.* New York: Barnes & Noble, 2005.

———. *The Works of John Bunyan.* Edited by George Offor. Glasgow: Blackie and Son, 1858.

Burge Gary M., and Andrew E. Hill, eds., *The Baker Illustrated Bible Commentary.* Grand Rapids: Baker, 2012.

Burroughs, Jeremiah. *The Rare Jewel of Christian Contentment.* Edinburgh: Banner of Truth, 1964.

Calvin, John. *Commentary on the Book of Acts.* Translated by Henry Beveridge. Grand Rapids: Christian Classics Ethereal Library, 2005.

———. *Institutes of the Christian Religion.* Translated by Henry Beveridge. Grand Rapids: Eerdmans, 1997.

Campbell, Duncan. "When God Stepped Down." Accessed June 19, 2018. https://media.sermonaudio.com/mediapdf/91088123510.pdf.

Dod, Albert B. *Essays: Theological and Miscellaneous.* New York: Wiley and Putnam, 1847.

Edwards, Jonathan. *Jonathan Edwards on Revival.* Carlisle, PA: Banner of Truth, 2014.

———. *The Life and Diary of David Brainerd.* Chicago: Moody, 1980.

———. *Religious Affections.* Carlisle, PA: Banner of Truth, 1997.

Gill, John. "John Gill's Exposition of the Whole Bible: Psalms 34." Studylight.org. Accessed January 2, 2018. https://www.studylight. org/commentaries/geb/psalms-34.html.

Graham, Billy. "Billy Graham: What is Repentance?" YouTube. Accessed January 2, 2018. https://youtu.be/irRjydQYVVY.

Henry, Matthew. *Matthew Henry's Commentary on the Whole Bible.* Peabody, MA: Hendrickson, 1996.

James, William. *The Varieties of Religious Experience.* New York: Random House, 1929.

Leclerc Brothers, dir. *Divided.* St. Chicopee, MA: Leclerc Brothers Motion Pictures, 2010. DVD.

Lewis, C. S. *Mere Christianity.* New York: Harper Collins, 1952.

Luther, Martin. *Luther's Works.* St. Louis: Concordia, 1960.

Machen, J. Gresham. *Christianity and Liberalism.* New York: MacMillan, 1923.

Murray, Iain H. *The Invitation System.* Carlisle: Banner of Truth Trust, 2002.

Nichols, William C., ed. *Seeking God: Jonathan Edwards' Evangelism Contrasted with Modern Methodologies.* Ames, Iowa: International Outreach, 2001.

North American Mission Board. "3 Circles: Life Conversation Guide." Life on Mission. Accessed December 9, 2018. http://lifeonmission book.com/conversation-guide.

Packer, J. I. *Evangelism and the Sovereignty of God.* Downers Grove, IL: Intervarsity, 2008.

Phillips, Richard D. *What's So Great about the Doctrines of Grace?* Sanford, FL: Reformation Trust, 2008.

Pink, A. W. *An Exposition of the Sermon on the Mount.* Grand Rapids: Baker, 1995.

Piper, John. *Does God Desire All to Be Saved?* Wheaton: Crossway Books, 2013.

———. "Going Hard after the Holy God." DesiringGod. Accessed December 29, 2017. http://www.desiringgod.org/sermons/going-hard-after-the-holy-god.

Ravenhill, Leonard. *Why Revival Tarries.* Zachary, LA: Fires of Revival, 1972.

Reidhead, Paris. "Ten Shekels and a Shirt." Paris Reidhead Bible Teaching Ministries. Accessed December 29, 2017. http://www.parisreidhead bibleteachingministries.org/Ten_Shekels_and_A_Shirt.html.

Religious Affections Ministries. Accessed June 19, 2018. http://religiousaffections.org.

Scougal, Henry. *The Life of God in the Soul of Man.* N.p.: Rough Draft Publishing, 2012.

Sibbes, Richard. *The Bruised Reed.* Edinburgh: Banner of Truth, 2011.

Spurgeon, Charles. "Repentance unto Life." Sermon No. 44. The Spurgeon Center. Accessed December 21, 2017. https://www.spurgeon.org/resource-library/sermons.

———. "Turn or Burn." Sermon No. 106. The Spurgeon Center. Accessed December 21, 2017. https://www.spurgeon.org/resource-library/sermons.

Walton, John H., Victor H. Matthews, and Mark W. Chavalas. *The IVP Bible Background Commentary: Old Testament.* Downers Grove, IL: Intervarsity, 2000.

Watson, Thomas. *The Doctrine of Repentance.* Carlisle: Banner of Truth, 2011.

Whitefield, George. "The Method of Grace." In Christian Classics Ethereal Library. Accessed January 6, 2018. www.ccel.org/ccel/whitefield/sermons.lx.html.

Made in the USA
Columbia, SC
01 February 2019